Country
QUILTS

Country
QUILTS

LINDA SEWARD

Photography by James Merrell

MITCHELL BEAZLEY

For Emily

Edited and designed by Mitchell Beazley International Ltd
Michelin House, 81 Fulham Road, London SW3 6RB

Design Director **Jacqui Small**
Executive Editor **Judith More**
Senior Art Editor **Larraine Lacey**
Junior Editor **Catherine Smith**
Editorial Assistant **Jaspal Bhangra**
Production **Sarah Schuman**

A CIP record for this book is available from the British Library

ISBN 1 85732 933 3

The publishers have made every effort to ensure that all instructions given
in this book are accurate and safe, but they cannot accept liability for any
resulting injury, damage or loss to either person or property whether direct
or consequential and howsoever arising. The author and publishers will be
grateful for any information which will assist them in keeping future
editions up to date.

*Cover quilt: A glowing mid-19th century quilt from New
York State; the maker of this rare piece may have taken
her inspiration from the delightfully named Lady Fingers
and Sunflowers design or Whig's Defeat.*

Page 1: A 19th-century red and white Pineapple quilt.

*Page 2: On the left is a stack of early 19th-century English
quilts; the picture on the right shows a selection of brilliantly
coloured Provençal quilts.*

*Right: An Ohio Star quilt hangs on the rough-hewn wooden
railing of a rustic porch.*

Typeset in Baskerville 3 Roman 12/16pt. and 11/16pt.
by Litho Link Ltd, Welshpool, Powys, Wales
Index compiled by Indexing Specialists, Hove, East Sussex
Origination by Scantrans Pte Ltd, Singapore
Produced by Mandarin Offset
Printed and bound in Hong Kong

Contents

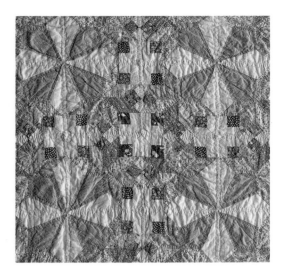

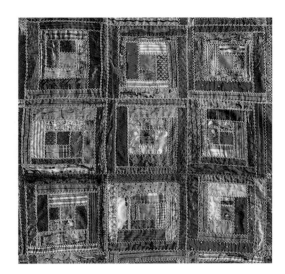

Introduction

A quilt epitomizes country style like no other single object – where something that was born of necessity has been turned into an art form. Start to decorate with quilts and you will marvel at the ease with which you can give a featureless room a focus and a feeling of warmth.

Why does a quilt have such a powerful effect? Perhaps it is because, by its very nature, a quilt is an incredibly personal object. Look at an antique example and you can almost feel the presence of the woman who made it so long ago. Study the quilt closely. See the tiny stitches sewn by hands that may now be still, but which performed hundreds of tasks, perhaps none more important than making this quilt.

Today, quilts are inseparable from country-style decorating and there are a host of ways in which you can use them to brighten your home. As you examine the quilts in this book you may decide that you would like to either buy or make your own quilt. If you have had some quiltmaking experience, you can try making one of the dozen quilts that can be found in the Projects section, starting on page 67; these are suitable for intermediate to very experienced quiltmakers. Complete step-by-step instructions and full-size templates and quilting patterns are given for each of these quilts.

However, you may decide that you'd rather purchase an antique quilt to decorate your home. If this is your chosen path, the following pages will give you some suggestions about where to begin.

The Turkey Tracks quilt draped on the split rail fence shows many years of wear, yet still retains a sense of dignity. Dating from around 1880, it was made in Knox County, Tennessee, of linsey, a hand-woven cloth of wool and cotton, so named because it originally had linen as the warp thread. It is unusual to find an intricate quilt in this fabric because linsey fabric unravels easily which limited quilt-makers to large, simple blocks.

Introduction

A Whig's Defeat quilt rests on a traditional cannonball bed (Atlanta Historical Society).

Broken Dishes, Ohio Star and Churn Dash are patriotic quilts in red, white and blue.

Resting on the wooden chairs are a Nosegay quilt and a Sawtooth Variation quilt.

Buying an antique quilt

Quilts have been going up in value for about the last 20 years. Gone are the days when you can walk into a junk shop and find a textile treasure for a very low price. Superlative antique quilts are commanding six-figure prices at auctions, and it isn't unusual to pay a five-figure sum for an old Amish quilt. So do you even have a hope of buying a lovely quilt at a reasonable price? The answer is definitely yes, but you have to know what you want and be able to recognize a well-made quilt.

Bargain quilts may still be found at flea markets, garage sales and auctions, but take great care in examining the quilt to make sure that it is in good condition. More expensive but probably higher in quality are the quilts for sale in quilt shops, antique shops and through quilt dealers. If you are serious about buying a quilt, here are some observations that you should make before parting with your money.

As you look at a quilt, your very first impression will be a visual one. This is created by the design elements and the fabrics from which the quilt is fashioned. Simply look at the quilt for a while to see whether you could live with it. If you genuinely like it, curb your impulse to buy the quilt until you have inspected its quality.

Examine the quilt's construction. Seams should be flat and unobtrusive. If any seams are incomplete or the edges not sufficiently fastened, make sure that you can fix the flaws without distrubing the rest of the quilt. Hand-sewn quilts are more valuable than those sewn on a machine.

Patchwork quilts should be well-pieced with matching seams and smoothly fitting pieces. For very expensive "best" quilts (see page 110), check that points have not been cut off by another seam and that corners meet precisely. Quilts that have a folk-art quality will often be irregularly pieced, which, in the view of many quilt enthusiasts, adds to their appeal. As a general rule, the more intricate the piecing, the more valuable the quilt.

On an appliquéd quilt, the appliqués must be sewn firmly in place with all the raw edges hidden. Appliqués should lie flat on the background without creases, pleats or other distortions. Look at the points and angled areas to make sure that they are well-executed. Curves should be smooth and flowing. The stitches on a hand-appliquéd quilt should be invisible unless they are meant to be decorative. On a machine-appliquéd quilt, if the edges have been turned under and secured with a straight line of sewing, see that the curves are smooth; if satin-stitching has been used, make sure that all raw edges of the appliqués are covered completely and that the ends are secured so that the stitching doesn't unravel.

Check the sashing (the strips of fabric between the blocks) and borders, if the quilt has any. They should be firmly sewn to the rest of the quilt, and ought to be relatively straight – although despite these warnings, many a quilt has been bought because of the charm of crooked sashing and borders!

Next look at the fabrics. Check for any obvious frays or tears in the quilt top, back or binding. If the quilt is stained, try to ascertain if the stains are permanent or whether they can be removed through cleaning. Look at the fabrics to see that they are appropriate to the overall appearance of the quilt, or if some look out of place, perhaps because they were added at a later time. An antique quilt that has been altered in some way will be of lower value than one that hasn't been touched. Quilts that are in pristine condition are the most sought-after and will generally command the highest prices.

For all quilts, but particularly wholecloth quilts, the quilting stitches should be small and even, and there must be enough quilting to hold the layers firmly together. The quilting ought to look as if it has been executed by one person and should look good on the back and the front. Pattern markings must not be obvious. An exception would be the blue markings on Durham quilts stamped by Elizabeth Sanderson (see page 122); if authenticated, these markings may actually add to the value of a North Country quilt.

Study the back of the quilt. The fabric should be of good quality, and if it is pieced, it should be well done. Then, examine the edges of the quilt. The binding should look as if it is of the same date as the rest of the quilt – many aged quilts have new bindings which really detract from their appearance. Different edge finishes such as piping, scallops or prairie points can add a great deal to the value of a quilt if they are well done.

Finally, see if you can find out about the history of the quilt – who made it, where was it made, and was it made for a reason such as a birth or wedding. Knowing a quilt's history will not only add to its value, but will also add to your pleasure in owning this small piece of the past.

People will certainly have different criteria for starting their own quilt collection, particularly if the end use is basically decorative. Noted quilt collector and historian Susan Jenkins has this advice for new collectors: "First, only buy what you really love; the quilt must have great appeal to you personally. Second, buy one that excels in a certain area – such as a quilt with a strong graphic design or one with an overall sense of harmony and balance. Third, make sure that the quilt is well executed by studying the details – the stitching, the fabrics, the border and the binding."

A pair of Honeycomb patchwork quilts have been hung in place of doors on this wardrobe.

Turkey red and sprigged prints comprise an early American patchwork sampler quilt.

A bright Lemoyne Star quilt can be seen through an Adirondack-style railing.

QUILTS IN THE HOME

Living Rooms

A country living room is a comfortable gathering place for family and friends, a room in which you can display treasured mementos – whether family heirlooms, special antique discoveries or hand-worked examples of your own craft – for your guests to enjoy. It is not a private room, but one which makes a statement about the way in which you prefer to live. Whether you are trying to recreate an authentic country-style room from a particular period or evoke a rustic feeling in a more informal way, a quilt can serve to complete the picture of well-worn history.

Quilts are an invaluable way to ring the changes in a decorative scheme. In winter, a country living room warmed by a robust log fire and furnished with richly coloured quilts is a cosy retreat from the chill outside. Pile on the layers generously; embellish walls and drape sofas with a collection of quilts, then make plump cushions or pillows in similar designs and matching colours. When summer comes, pack away your winter quilts and bring out lighter versions in pastel colours for a refreshing change.

Previous page: The Schoolhouse design evokes a country feeling like no other quilt pattern. This charming quilt was hand-pieced and tufted in Vermont around 1880.

Left: Quilts can serve to link different areas in a small studio into one cohesive unit. A T-Block quilt hangs from the gallery; it was made in Piedmont, North Carolina in 1920. A 1930s Tulip quilt from North Carolina draws the eye to the dining area down below. The living room chairs are upholstered in fabric printed with a Whig's Defeat design, available from Bob Timberlake (see the Directory).

A Bear's Paw quilt draped over an old chest provides both colour and a focus to this informal living room; it was made around 1920. The 1940s Friendship Star quilt tossed on a chair blends well with the weathered beams and stone floor; it was made by Mrs Edna Shoaf Dorsett in Davidson County, North Carolina.

A quilt can serve as a link between colour, pattern and texture in a room, and even one good piece, thoughtfully displayed, can make a room come alive. Attract attention to a dark corner by tossing a quilt on a chair or hanging one on a wall. Soften the hard lines of an austere room by featuring a quilt with patterned fabrics or a textured surface. A quilt pieced with an array of coloured fabrics can brighten a room that is painted in a neutral tone. A striking quilt will draw the eye across a large room and can be an effective conversation starter – this would be ideal in living rooms that will be used for entertaining.

The summer-weight Log Cabin quilt made at the turn of the century seems to echo the patterns in the colourful 1880s Navajo rugs. (For stockist of rugs and Indian baskets see the Directory: Furniture and Accessories, USA.) A Crazy patchwork cushion or pillow adds to the eclectic feeling in this Adirondack-style living room.

There is something intrinsically comforting about settling down on a sofa nestled in a soft quilt. Quilts bought specially for snuggling should be able to stand up to some wear and tear – they must be sturdily constructed, well-stitched and without flaws that would be exacerbated by everyday usage. The stout-hearted reliability of a practical quilt adds character to a decorating scheme. You should save the more fragile antique quilts for display in areas that are not subject to so much use. Alternatively, you can make your own quilt to enhance your living room; choose one of the dozen designs featured in the second half of this book.

Living Rooms

If you are looking for a refreshing way to decorate a country-style living room, take your design cue from a recognizable motif on a favourite quilt. Quilts that feature baskets, stars or flowers can be the basis for a subtle but effective decorating theme. If you have a lovely Basket quilt, for example, start a collection of small ceramic or metal basket ornaments, choose upholstery fabrics printed in a complementary design, or stencil simple images of baskets on walls and floors. Then display a few baskets in unexpected places around the room. Although the finished result may contain a variety of colours, textures and patterns, the decor will be tied together by a single dominant motif – baskets.

Previous page: Rag rugs, Navajo Indian weavings and patchwork quilts work together to create a cheery and cohesive decor in this New England living room. A 19th century Sampler quilt from Texas rests on the arm of a 1930s hide-covered chair that was found on a Montana dude ranch.

Right: The Courthouse Square quilt folded on the back of the sofa was made in Ohio around 1890. A quilt featuring an unusual cross variation is draped on the back of the chair; it has an inner border of sawteeth and was made around 1860 in New England. Cotton seeds are visible through the fine cotton material when the quilt is held up to the light.

Below: Set against the rich leather of the sofa and the warm wooden walls, an Octagonal Star quilt glows with colour.

Kitchens and Dining Rooms

The heart of the home is said to be in the kitchen, and perhaps nowhere is this more true than in a country home. The warmth of the hearth and the aroma of good cooking serve as a magnet to draw people together for food and conversation. Country style needn't be sacrificed for the sake of convenience; weathered wood and homespun fabrics will blend comfortably with sympathetically chosen appliances. The decorating plan can include all types of furnishings that wouldn't normally be associated with kitchens and dining rooms: quilts are a prime example.

Install a discreet extractor fan or ventilator hood if you don't have generous windows you can fling open to usher in fresh air, and then you won't need to fret over the effects of cooking smells on your quilts.

While it is not recommended that you actually use a quilt as a tablecloth during a meal, covering an unused table with a quilt is an excellent way to turn the heart of your home into a cozy and inviting place. If you'd like to use a quilt as a tablecloth, protect the top with lightweight Plexiglas (heavier plastic or glass might leave marks). Or throw a clear sheet of plastic over the quilt for meals.

Set against a backdrop of weathered wood, an 1840s quilt, made in New York State, provides a strong accent. The quilt's elegant appearance is contradicted by its name – Toad in a Puddle! The curtains can be drawn against the sun to keep the quilt from fading.

Above: The eclectic furnishings in this dining room are unified by the soft colours of the child-sized Cotton Reel quilt, dating from the early 1800s. Peeping out from underneath is an indigo Jacob's Ladder summer counterpane.

Right: Friendly and informal, this country kitchen is enlivened by the sturdy patchwork quilt on the table; it was bought at a New England auction for just $2.75! Another typical 1930s quilt is folded over a ladderback chair.

There are other ways that you can use quilts in your kitchen or dining room without placing them on a table or chair. Have a small quilt professionally framed in Plexiglas to protect it from kitchen smells and splashes; it can then be safely hung on the wall. Alternatively, it is not unusual to find individual antique quilt blocks for sale; many of these were made as samples, others might have been made for a quilt that was never finished. If you acquire one, mount it on acid-free rag board covered with cotton fabric. Then frame it in Plexiglas, allowing air space between the fabric and the plastic; make sure air is allowed to circulate around the block. A grouping of framed blocks would create a striking impact in a room. Or you can sew quilt blocks yourself for framing; you can try designs such as Cake Stand, Sugar Bowl or Fruit Basket.

You can also use quilt designs as part of your decorative scheme. You could cover chair cushions with patchwork, or appliqué simple designs on placemats, napkins or curtains. Your kitchen may have an unsightly undercounter storage space; why not make a patchwork skirt to conceal what's underneath. If you like the look of glass-fronted cupboards, but prefer to keep the contents out of sight, consider lining the inside of the doors with patchwork or appliquéd fabric.

If you are having an outdoor party, it would be charming to drape quilts over bannisters and railings to make your guests feel welcome. However, you must never expose quilts to direct sunlight for an extended period. It would be best to position the quilts in dappled sunlight or shade.

Quilted accessories can strike a country mood in almost any setting, but you do not have to be a sewing expert in order to decorate your country kitchen or dining room in this way. Many patchwork and appliqué designs can be easily adapted for another decorative country craft: stencilling. The stencils can be used to decorate floors, walls or doors. If that works successfully, you can go on to stencil tablecloths, napkins and placemats with matching or contrasting patterns.

Previous page: Twin tables are garnished with quilts featuring motifs inspired by nature. The Tulip appliqué quilt on the left was made in the late 1800s in Davidson County, North Carolina. The Tree of Life on the right is elaborately quilted with feathers on a grid of squares; it was made in Pennsylvania around 1920. The Crib quilt in the basket was also made in Pennsylvania around 1850.

Left: The Lone Star quilt on the table dates from around 1930 and was made in Missouri; the diamond patchwork binding is an unusual touch. The humble Churn Dash quilt on the back of the sofa provides a dramatic splash of dark colour.

Below: A Broken Dishes quilt is possibly not the most appropriate design to feature on a dining room table! The Honeycomb patchwork on the chairs adds an informal touch.

Bedrooms

A country bedroom is a comfortable sanctuary from the outside world. Lying warm and snug beneath a handmade quilt, it is easy to forget the day's troubles in this most private of rooms. However, the bedroom has not always been a peaceful, secluded haven.

In the early days when people lived in one-room houses, sleeping mats and bedding were simply pushed to one side of the main room until required. Once houses developed to the point where the bedroom became a separate room, it was often shared by an entire family. The main bed was wide to accommodate several people, and whoever couldn't fit in bed with the parents would sleep either on a trundle bed which was stored underneath and pulled out for nighttime use, or on cushions or pillows and sleeping mats arranged on the floor. In order to cover this sleeping family heap, early quilts were very large indeed; it was not uncommon for a quilt to be nine feet square! In the morning, the trundle would be pushed back underneath the main bed, and the mats and cushions or pillows piled on top of the bed. These were covered over during the day by the large quilt. As homes became more subdivided and individual bedrooms proliferated, quilts became smaller and more rectangular, but were still made in great abundance.

It then became common for a woman to feature her best quilts on the "company" beds in her guest bedroom. She would carefully arrange the quilts so that when her guests went in for the night, they would have to peel off the quilts, layer by layer, before they could retire. In so doing, of course, they couldn't help admiring the skillful handiwork that went into making each quilt.

This Seven Stars quilt was made around 1850 by the owner's great-great-great grandmother, Nancy Millar Alley, a pioneer woman who migrated to Texas in 1830.

The iron bedstead in this exceptionally pretty Victorian bedroom is decorated with antique tablecloths, sheets and quilts.

The centrepiece of a lovely Colonial bedroom is the 19th-century bed with its original Meandering Vine appliqué quilt.

The simple patchwork quilt on the Elizabethan four-poster bed marries well with other hand-worked textiles, like the Queen Anne crewel hangings and the kelim.

A Honeycomb patchwork quilt provides a pool of colour against plain white walls and the rustic twig headboard of an American Adirondack-style bed.

The dark tones of the Georgian furniture contrast well with the pale patchwork and appliqué quilts.

A magnificently quilted 19th-century Durham quilt has a twisted undulating feather design filled in with a grid of crosshatching.

The focal point of an ethnic-style bedroom is an elaborate and colourful Gujerat bridal canopy from Northern India which serves as a lightweight pieced quilt.

The Double Tulip quilt on the canopy bed echoes the colours of another, called Posies Round the Square, draped over the table. A small, easy-to-launder cloth protects the table quilt.

Above: Antique toys collected by the small residents of this bedroom are displayed with pride. The twin maple beds, made around 1800, sport a 19th century Goose Chase quilt on the right and a Diamond in a Square quilt on the left, an example of how quilts with different designs can work well together.

Right: A red and white Double Irish Chain quilt echoes the red centre squares of the Log Cabin quilt displayed on the authentic rope bed which dates back to around 1880. A red stepback cupboard holds the owners' collection of early homespun fabrics, which may have been used to make some of the quilts in their collection!

Although quilts were originally made as mere bedcovers, they evolved into much more than that. A woman's most highly prized attribute was her skill with a needle, and this everyday activity turned bedcovers into works of art that were admired by family and friends, and later, achieved recognition at country fairs and contests. But quilts reverted back to their original practical status as women in America began moving West in the mid-19th century. Quilts served many functions along the way. They were used to pack precious dishes and other breakable objects, they were folded to act as cushions on the hard wooden seats of covered wagons during the journey, they were used to protect the sides of the wagons during Indian attacks and they served as the family's bedding at night. More sombrely, quilts were also used to bury the dead. It was very common for one or more members of a family to perish during the arduous journey West. Accidents, attacks from Indians, illness and the lack of medical attention combined with the fact that time couldn't be taken to stop and nurse a sick person back to health contributed to the high mortality rate of both young and old. Heartbreaking though it was, families were forced to bury their loved ones where they died, in unmarked graves that they hoped would be overlooked by the Indians and subsequent travellers. Rather than leave the corpse alone in an unmourned grave, the pioneers wrapped it in one of their best quilts, so that they would have the comfort of knowing they had left a little bit of themselves behind with their loved one. When the pioneers finally arrived at their destination, they were very grateful to have their remaining quilts around to remind them of the life they had left and the family and friends that they would never see again.

Square in a Square blocks are arranged in bars on this 1880s quilt made in Tennessee; the patchwork design is also known as Twelve Diamonds. Typical of the late 19th-century farm houses in eastern Tennessee, the furniture includes a four-poster rope bed with a trundle bed underneath for a child. The floor is covered with home-made rugs braided from strips of cloth. Typical work overalls and hats as well as prized family photographs are hung on the walls. Farmers in the hills of East Tennessee continued subsistence farming well into the 1940s when the benefits of electricity and improved roads finally reached them.

This utilitarian Crazy Quilt harmonizes well with the brightly coloured rag carpet. The quilt is assembled in blocks which help to unify the design; it was made around 1910 from a muted palette of cotton and woollen fabrics. The reverse side is made of patchwork squares and the only frivolous touch is the single daisy appliquéd onto one of the patches. Forest materials furnish this room in Bull Cottage, which forms part of the Adirondack Museum in upper New York State (see the Directory). A bed with a headboard of applied bark, a night table decorated in twig and bark, a woven hickory rocker and a deer hoof footstool are the essence of American rustic style.

Previous page: Invitingly heaped with pillows, an Adirondack-style twig bed flaunts a 19th century Nine-Patch Variation quilt, with a contrasting quilt in turkey red and white folded at its foot. A simple doll's quilt from the early 1900s hangs on the wall.

Left: Fresh flowers and painted latticework harmonize with an 1860s English quilt to give this guest bedroom the feeling of a gentle summer's day. Composed of men's shirting and sprigged print fabrics, it is typical of the everyday quilts made in the mid-19th century.

Above left: Soft pastel lavender and crisp white fabrics comprise this charming Double Irish Chain quilt made in New Jersey around 1930. Floral wreaths are quilted in the white blocks between the "chains", while the chain itself is outline-quilted.

Above right: Its colours softened by time, a Dogwood quilt gives a nostalgic appeal to a guest bedroom. The pieced ice cream cone border is typical of the quilts made during the Depression in the United States. Unusual edge finishes add value to a quilt if well done.

Quilts offer a practical, colourful way to enliven a bedroom. If you are going out to buy an antique quilt specially to feature on a bed, there are several criteria you should keep in mind. First, make a note of the size of quilt you are looking for – there is no point in buying one that is either too small or too large for your bed. If the bed is positioned in the middle of the room, the quilt should have enough of an overhang on each side to cover the bottom edge of the mattress. Quilts that are square in shape are very common, and this may work best for a wide bed without a footboard. If your bed has a footboard, you might consider buying a quilt with cut-out corners – these quilts were specifically made for four-poster beds.

If you are going to actually sleep beneath the quilt, it will occasionally need to be washed. First, check to see whether the quilt you are thinking of buying has ever been washed at all. You can tell if the quilt has been washed because the fabric will be slightly puckered around the quilting stitches. Also, the padding inside the quilt may be slightly bunched rather than lying in a smooth layer. If the quilt shows no evidence of having been cleaned, washing will seriously devalue it; you may be better off buying a quilt that has seen some use and has already been cleaned. If the quilt you wish to buy has definitely been washed, study the fabric to ascertain whether it will continue to wash and wear well: the material should be closely woven and the piece well quilted so that the padding inside doesn't shift as it is cleaned.

Should you go to a quilt dealer or a shop specializing in antique quilts, you can be faced with a bewildering array of beautiful quilts and may feel confused about where to begin. Your price constraints will automatically eliminate some quilts, and you may be able to narrow the field further by seeking one in a particular colourway. See pages 10-11 for more advice on how to buy an antique quilt.

Below: Quilts in complementary colours provide strong accents to the white walls and dark beams in this attic guest bedroom. The Rocky Road to Kansas string quilt in the foreground has been well used. A striking 1930s Broken Dishes quilt graces the other bed; it contains a catalogue of 1930s prints, mainly geometric, and is quilted in a wave and seashell quilting pattern.

Right: A turkey red and white appliqué quilt echoes the warm red of the painted walls in this original 1830s Texas home. The traditional pattern is called Oak Leaf and Reel, but because of the additional fleur de lis appliqués between the blocks, it almost has the appearance of a "Robbing Peter to Pay Paul" design. The rag rugs introduce additional colour to the stark wooden floors.

You can never have too many quilts in a bedroom. Pile quilts on beds several layers deep, hang them on walls, drape them over chairs and night tables or fold them for display in a chest. Find or make bright patchwork and appliqué cushions and pillows to heap on the bed in a casual jumble; look for small doll quilts that can be displayed on top of dressers. Quilts that have been slightly damaged can be folded to conceal the worn areas and placed at the foot of the bed. Whether you are looking for a quilt to use as a soft accent or as the focus of attention in a country-style bedroom, you will be spoiled for choice.

Left: Drunkard's Path is traditionally associated with the Women's Christian Temperance Union; this example in indigo blue and white was made in Vermont around 1890. It is teamed with a Sunburst Variation quilt made in Appalachia around the same time. In this quilt, indigo sunbursts with yellow middles are set in circular blocks surrounded by a zigzag border.

Below: A child's pieced and appliquéd quilt made in North Carolina is draped over the rail of the little wooden bed. Most of the appliqués are edged with decorative stitching; 1926 has been embroidered in one corner.

Displaying Quilts

Until 1971, when the first major quilt exhibition took place at the Whitney Museum of American Art in New York City, quilts weren't perceived as anything other than bed coverings. However, for this exhibition, the curators decided to hang the quilts on walls. Suddenly, people realized that a quilt could also be a glorious example of abstract art or folk art. It was as a direct result of this watershed exhibition that quilts spread beyond the bedroom.

Once you have decided to decorate your home with quilts, you'll find that your options are limited only by your imagination. Quilts are versatile objects, and if treated with respect, can last for many years and give you great enjoyment at the same time. Be sure to read the section on *Conservation*, beginning on page 133, if you have any questions about your ideas for displaying a quilt.

You should not display a quilt in the same position indefinitely. As a general rule, quilts should be allowed to rest for the same amount of time that they have been on display. You should fold the quilt and store it horizontally as directed on page 137 to allow the fibres to rest. There is a positive aspect to this restriction — you can add variety to your decorative theme every so often as you rotate your collection of quilts.

The sturdy Bordered Star quilt from Durham is in the style of Elizabeth Sanderson, who may have marked it. It is hung from its top edge by a series of clips; this type of fixing method is not recommended for very fragile quilts which can be damaged by the weight of the hanging (see How to Hang a Quilt on page 139). The colours are echoed in the Strippy Sawtooth quilt on the daybed. The seat is well-padded with some white Durham quilts.

Displaying Quilts

Above: The 1930s doll quilt on the buttermilk blue schoolmaster's desk was made from wool scraps and tied with yarn. The fabric doll and teddy bears are a charming accent to the blue wicker sewing basket and the owners' collection of old books.

Right: A Double-Nine Patch quilt graces the Adirondack-style twig bed, while a Variable Star quilt is folded at its foot. An unusual variation of an Irish Chain quilt hangs over the door of a chest containing many more quilts. The easy country atmosphere is enhanced by a comfortable jumble of patchwork pillows on the bed and the patchwork bear and pillow that share the ladderback chair.

Quilts that are *folded and stacked* in a chest will convey the impression of a generous collection and add colour and interest to any room. However, the combined weight of the upper quilts can cause those at the bottom of the pile to be put under excessive pressure. If you are featuring your quilts this way, periodically rotate the position of the quilts in the stack, refolding each one every time you do this. Wood can be acidic, so if the quilts are in a wooden chest, protect them by placing a barrier of acid-free paper or cotton fabric between the quilts and the wood. Arrange the quilts on the shelves so that they complement each other in colour and texture.

Displaying Quilts

Above: Partly folding a quilt for display on a chair or table can artfully conceal areas of the piece which may be damaged. The Half Moon Rising design was made in South Carolina at the turn of the century. The woollen Welsh quilt folded on the ottoman is a Variable Star design with Prince of Wales feather quilting and traditional Welsh spirals; it dates from 1880.

Right: A look of casual informality is achieved by tossing these lovely turkey-red and white quilts over the 18th-century stickback chairs. The Durham Basket quilt on the left dates from around 1900 and was quilted by Elizabeth Sanderson. The unusual Circles and Crescents quilt on the right was made around 1850, also in Durham. An early painted Delft rack holds a collection of spongeware.

An easy way to exhibit a quilt is on a *quilt rack*; this is an ideal means to show off an old quilt that may not be strong enough to hang on a wall, but which has a striking pattern that would be hidden if it were merely folded. If your quilt has damaged areas you can hide them by carefully folding and arranging the quilt on a rack.

You don't actually need to invest in special display furniture like quilt racks or storage chests, however, because a quilt will look equally well draped over the back of a simple wooden chair. If you have railings, beams or galleried areas in your home, you are fortunate to possess "built-in" quilt racks. If you have an unsightly metal radiator that is no longer in use but is too expensive to remove, try arranging a quilt over it to make it into a feature. Or rejuvenate an old chest by covering it with a quilt.

Hanging a quilt on a wall is the most obvious way to display a textile other than on a bed. If you are going to display a quilt on a wall, you must make sure that the quilt isn't too old and that it is sturdily constructed so that the pressure of hanging doesn't cause sagging or deterioration. When you buy a quilt to feature on a wall, you need to think about it in the same way you would consider a painting you were thinking of buying. The quilt's design will be of primary importance. Study the border carefully, as it will serve to frame the quilt on the wall. Hanging a quilt against a wall that delicately echoes one of the quilt's own colours will bring out the best in both. Pay special attention to shaped quilts which will need extra support. Never hang a quilt above a mantel unless the fireplace is not in use.

Overleaf: A magnificent Lone Star quilt successfully competes with the Tennessee woods surrounding the deck of this country home; it was made in Memphis around 1880. The Tumbling Blocks quilt, on the left, was made around 1900 in North Carolina from cotton fabrics. The early 19th century rainbow prints featured in the Sunburst quilt, on the right, are much older than the 1874 date quilted into its surface; it was made in West Virginia. Some of the owners' collection of whirligigs are also on view.

Top Left: A small nook is transformed into a display area featuring a Four Pointed Star quilt covering a low chest.

Bottom Left: An unused radiator cloaked with a magnificent silk Star of Bethlehem quilt acts as a shelf for the owner's antique English quilts.

Far Left: The colours of America's Union Army are emblazoned on this Carpenter's Square variation quilt, made around 1860; it covers a sideboard.

Left: Bright ceramic dishes complement the jaunty sailboats in this patchwork wall hanging that originates from Milwaukee, Wisconsin. The quilt was made in 1939 by the W.P.A. Handicraft Project, an organization that provided jobs for the unemployed.

Above: An unusual Honeycomb patchwork wall hanging is probably the middle of a quilt that was never finished. When hanging a shaped quilt, extra care must be taken to show it to its best advantage. In this case, a sleeve was sewn across the widest part of the quilt; a strip of wood was inserted through the sleeve to take the weight of the wall hanging. Velcro was sewn to the top of the quilt back and fastened to another piece of Velcro stapled to a flat piece of wood secured to the wall.

Soft Furnishings

Well-chosen soft furnishings can provide the finishing touches to all the rooms in your country-style home. Heap a mountain of patchwork pillows on a bed to emphasize the comforting cocoon you have created in your rustic bedroom. Soften the austere furnishings of a period living room with cushions of richly quilted Provençal fabrics. Give a face-lift to a well-worn sofa by tossing a sturdy quilt on top to hide sagging springs. And if the fabric on your favourite overstuffed chair doesn't quite match the rest of the room, drape it with a quilt in just the right colours. You can change the mood of your room to match the seasons by simply switching quilts – flamboyant appliquéd florals in spring and summer can give way to a patchwork of warm, rich wools in autumn and winter.

Think about displaying quilts in spontaneous ways. A child-size quilt would be a naive and charming alternative to a table runner. Frame a collection of patchwork blocks for a simple yet bright solution to a dark hallway. A ladderback chair acting as a perch for a patchwork teddy bear could add an artless touch to an odd corner. By their very nature, quilted accessories invite you to feel them, to study them and to enjoy their quirkiness and innocent qualities. Use them to add a feeling of honesty and sincerity to your country-style decor.

A collection of patchwork and appliqué pillows rests on top of a child-size Log Cabin quilt; the quilt is composed of a variety of nutbrown calicos which give it a warm glow, but which make it very fragile as the dyes have caused the fabrics to deteriorate. The red and white patchwork pillow is in a classic Single Irish Chain pattern. A primitive teddy bear has been appliquéd on the heart-shaped cushion.

Soft Furnishings

There is a great deal of controversy in the quilting world about cutting up old quilts and recycling them to make clothing or soft furnishings such as cushions, pillows and toys. When one well-known New York designer began doing this several years ago, there was such an outcry from antique quilt lovers that he actually gave it up, even though it would have been very profitable for him. To most quilt collectors, the idea of cutting up any quilt – antique or modern – is extremely painful.

With care, a tattered quilt can be repaired, or the damage contained and deterioration slowed to the minimum (see page 135). Even if a quilt is not physically repaired, it can be folded to conceal damaged areas, and used either as a throw on a chair or at the foot of a bed. If you have several quilts on display in a chest, it is easy to fold a frayed quilt to show off its best qualities and hide the deteriorating portion. A worn-out quilt is a faithful friend, and should be treated with respect. Keeping quilts in their original form is the only way we have of preserving their history and that of the women who made them.

However, there are people who believe that if most of a quilt is ruined beyond repair, there is nothing wrong with cutting away the usable portions to give them a new life in another form. The thinking behind this is that a quilt is by nature a recycled product, and that women of the past thought nothing of using one of *their* old quilts as the padding for a new one. However, the reason for this can easily be explained: in the past women didn't cherish their utilitarian quilts as we do today, nor did they consider their quilts as historical objects. However, if it were possible to interview the original maker of a tattered quilt, we might find that she would actually prefer her quilt to be recycled rather than left unused in a drawer for historical purposes.

Recycling an antique quilt is a very personal decision, and one that only you can make based on the condition of the individual quilt. If you are in any doubt, consult a conservator (see the Directory for a list of addresses).

A patriotic theme is the basis for the decoration of this breezy country-style porch in New York state. American flags reflect the colours of the antique quilt and newly made cushions and pillows. The red and white Delectable Mountains quilt on the bench is kept well out of the sunlight to avoid fading. A Schoolhouse pillow on the chair accentuates the red of the chrysanthemums. The gypsy willow furniture from Arkansas is available from the T. P. Saddle Blanket & Trading Co. (see the Directory). The birdhouses were made by a folk artist while he was spending some time in jail during the 1950s.

Top left: A 19th-century patchwork quilt pieced together from English dress prints is draped on a gingham chair. It features a variety of traditional star designs.

Top right: A fresh, pretty look has been achieved by covering an armchair with a quilt and cushions; the quilt's pink stripes are accentuated by their placement on the chair.

Left: Glowing red walls and faded hydrangeas are the perfect backdrop for this typical old English Strippy quilt, made around the turn of the century.

Above: An old ramshackle sofa has been concealed beneath a large utilitarian English quilt which has then been comfortably covered with a selection of cushions.

Above: A country-style ladderback chair holds a Victorian Crazy quilt and matching teddy bear, made around 1880 in Pennsylvania. Velvets, wools and cottons of all types were used in the construction of these pieces. A new patchwork-style teddy bear can be made using a commercial pattern; just construct a piece of patchwork fabric large enough to accommodate the pattern pieces. Button eyes and a matching bow will give the toy its own personality.

Above: A woollen quilt, made around 1925, is backed with cotton flannel and tied with yarn; it may have been a child's first attempt at patchwork. The pillow is in a Windmill pattern.

Right: A Mennonite Octagon quilt made in a variety of rich, dark wools is relieved by the careful placement of pairs of white triangles which look like flying birds; it dates from around 1920.

Pillows and cushions are probably the most popular country-style accessories. Patchwork, appliqué or quilted, tossed on a sofa, piled on a bed or artfully arranged on a chair, they will add the perfect finishing touch to every room in the house.

It isn't difficult to make your own cushions and pillows. First select the fabric(s) for the front; you can make a patchwork or appliqué block or use a plain piece of fabric that can be quilted. If you are going to quilt the pillow front; cut a matching piece of batting/wadding and a piece of plain unbleached fabric for the bottom layer; assemble the three layers for quilting as described on page 130, then quilt the front as desired.

For the back of the cushion, cut a piece of fabric the same height as the front and 13 mm/½ in wider; cut the fabric vertically about 5 cm/2 in from one short end for insertion of the zipper. Choose a matching zipper that is about 5 cm/2 in smaller in size than the cushion; insert the zipper between the cut edges of the back following the manufacturer's instructions.

Pin the back to the front with right sides facing and raw edges even; stitch together 6mm/¼in from the edges all around. Clip off each of the four corners at an angle, then turn right side out through the zipper opening. Insert a down pillow form slightly larger than the pillow through the zipper opening.

QUILT
PROJECTS

Patchwork Designs

With all the equipment and beautiful fabrics available today, as well as the leisure time to spend on a project, you'd think it would be easy to duplicate, if not surpass, the skills displayed on old quilts. But begin working on one of these designs and your respect for the woman who made it will grow with each seam that you sew. Consider that many of the women who made these quilts were uneducated in mathematics and geometry; how did they come up with these designs and then make them work? Then ponder the fact that the time for quilt-making was eked out from the hundreds of other tasks women were expected to accomplish every day; bone-weary they may have been, but they still had enough energy left at the end of the day to add a few stitches to their quilts.

Most of the quilts in this section have hundreds of pieces, so perhaps the most important aspect of successful patchwork is accuracy. Be accurate from the beginning – when you mark and cut out the fabrics. Stitch precisely, sewing the exact same seam allowance of 6mm/¼ in for all the pieces. Don't be afraid to unpick inaccurately sewn stitches which can throw out the regularity of the rest of the quilt.

If you want to make one of the designs that follow but are afraid to tackle an enormous project, try doubling the size of the design and making fewer blocks; the larger the pieces, the easier it is to sew them together.

Previous page: An 1890s Princess Feather quilt from North Carolina makes an elegant wall-hanging.

Right: Honeycomb quilts are quintessentially English. This one was made from dress fabrics around 1840.

Autograph Block

As the United States became more industrialized, 19th-century doomsday prophets deplored the emphasis on making money as being ruinous to society's moral fibre and the family in particular. It was felt that one way to inspire moral improvement was through the organization of societies and associations that would bring back old values. So a number of benevolent societies associated with women and the church were formed. Among these were the Women's Guilds, Ladies' Home Missionary Societies, Fancy Work Improvement Clubs and probably the most prevalent, the Ladies' Aid Societies. The tangible outcome of these societies was the needlework that was done for worthy causes. Quilts, in particular, were made to give to the poor, send to missionaries or to auction for some charitable purpose.

Signature or autograph quilts came into existence as a way for a society to raise money for a specific cause, usually related to the local church or school. Signees contributed anywhere from five cents to five dollars to autograph the quilt. Once the quilt was finished, it was then auctioned for additional funds, or given to a prominent local person. Fundraising quilts of this type were typically wholecloth quilts with turkey-red embroidered signatures, or patchwork quilts with a dominant red and white colour palette such as the one shown here which was made in North Carolina in 1913 for a church building fund. The documentation of the entire area in which an autograph quilt was made was often stitched onto its surface, inadvertently helping future historians.

The Autograph quilt on the bed is complemented by the elegant appliquéd Poppy quilt, which was made in Piedmont, North Carolina in 1905.

Patchwork Designs

Ability level : Intermediate

Size

Block: 30.4 cm/12 in square; 49 blocks required

Finished Quilt: 224.7 × 224.7 cm/88½ × 88½ in square

Materials

11¼ m/yds white fabric (includes fabric for quilt back, sashing and bias binding)

8¼ m/yds red fabric (includes fabric for quilt back and sashing posts)

226 × 226 cm/89 × 89 in piece of wadding/batting (includes seam allowance)

Templates for E: 3.2 × 31.7 cm/1¼ × 12½ in rectangle; F: 3.2 X 3.2 cm/ 1¼ × 1¼ in square (measurements include seam allowance)

Quilt Plan

Quilt Block

Cutting

Note: A 6 mm/¼ in seam allowance is included in all measurements; pattern pieces do not include a seam allowance.

Quilt Back: One central panel, 77.4 × 226 cm/30½ × 89 in, red fabric; 2 side panels, 76.2 × 226 cm/30 × 89 in, white fabric.

Bias Binding: From white fabric, cut one 111.7 cm/44 in square and one 30 cm/11 in square. Following the instructions for bias binding on p. 130, cut 4 cm/1½ in wide bias strips and sew together to measure 10 m/yds.

Sashing: 84 E sashing strips, white fabric; 36 F sashing posts, red fabric.

Note: If you were to cut out and sew each strip in this quilt individually, it would be very time-consuming. Save time by making striped fabric as directed on p.73. Then use A and B templates to cut out the required number of pieces from the striped fabric. For greatest accuracy, use a rotary cutter and rotary ruler to cut the strips; see p. 128. If you prefer using scissors, measure and mark fabrics with a ruler and pencil before cutting.

Red/White Striped Fabric (for A triangles): From the full width of the white fabric, cut 84 strips, each 3.2 cm/1¼ in wide. From the full width of the red fabric, cut 112 strips, each 3.2 cm/1¼ in wide. Following Step 1, sew 4 red and 3 white strips together, alternating colours. Construct 27 more red/white striped fabrics in the same manner.

White/Red Striped Fabric (for B rectangles): From the full width of the white fabric, cut 39 strips, each 2.7 cm/1¹⁄₁₆ in wide. From the full width of the red fabric, cut 39 strips, each 2.7 cm/1¹⁄₁₆ in wide. Following Step 2, sew 3 white and 3 red strips together, alternating colours. Construct 12 more white/red striped fabrics in the same manner.

Pattern Pieces: (Number of pieces for a single block are in parenthesis. See instructions, left, for making striped fabric; for a less graphic effect cut A, C and D from a dark fabric and B from a light fabric. Patterns are on p. 153.) A: (4) 196 red/white striped fabric; B: (4) 196 white/red striped fabric; C: (4) 196 red; D: (1) 49 white.

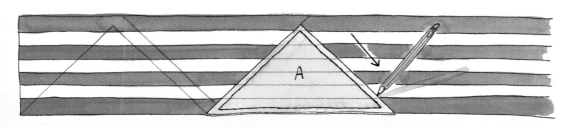

Piecing an Autograph Quilt Block

1 Make a template for A and use it to cut out the required number of pieces from the red/white striped fabric. Mark and cut only one layer at a time to prevent the striped fabric from stretching.

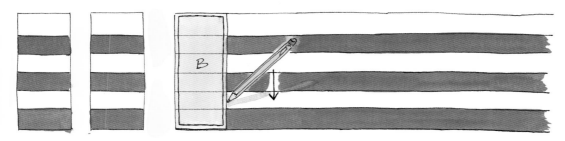

2 Make a template for B and use it to cut out the required number of pieces from the white/red striped fabric. Mark and cut only one layer at a time to prevent the striped fabric from stretching.

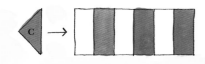

3 Sew a C triangle to the white end of a B rectangle. Repeat three times for a total of four B-C pieces.

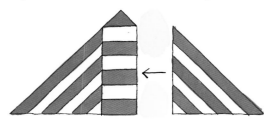

4 Sew an A triangle to each side of two B-C pieces.

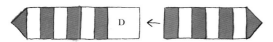

5 Sew B-C to each side of D for the central strip.

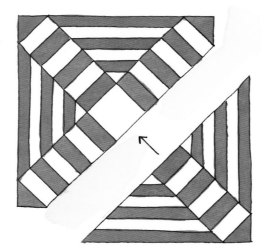

6 Sew the A-B-C triangles to each side of the central strip to complete the block.

7 Construct 48 more Autograph Quilt blocks in the same manner.

Assembling the Quilt

8 Following the Quilt Plan and working on a large flat surface, arrange the patchwork blocks with the E sashing strips and the F sashing posts.

9 Assemble the quilt top in horizontal rows. Following the Quilt Plan, sew seven patchwork blocks and six E sashing strips together to make the first row. Stitch six more rows of blocks and sashing together in the same manner.

10 Following the Quilt Plan, sew seven E sashing strips and 6 F sashing posts together to make a sashing row. Stitch five more rows of strips and posts together in the same manner.

11 Sew the rows of blocks and sashing together.

12 To construct the quilt back, sew a white side-panel to each long edge of the central red panel. Press the seam allowances toward the red panel.

13 Assemble the quilt top, wadding/batting and back as directed on page 130.

Finishing the Quilt

14 Outline-quilt the edges of each of the pieces, including the sashing and posts. Quilt an X across the middle of each D square.

15 Trim the four corners of the quilt into a gentle curve as shown in the photograph on p. 71.

16 Bind the quilt with a separate bias binding as directed on p. 131.

Whig's Defeat

From the time of the Revolutionary War, patriotic quilts were made by scores of women. Since they couldn't vote, these women were trying, in the way that they knew best, to make political statements. Events such as the presidential elections, the War of 1812, the Mexican War and the Civil War saw quiltmakers industriously stitching quilts that would disclose their political leanings and symbolize their opinions.

As the country evolved, political parties became powerful institutions in America. The Whig Party, which lasted from around 1832 to 1852, stood for the common man, while the Democrats represented the middle class. The Whigs saw victory in 1840, when General William Henry Harrison was elected President of the United States, with John Tyler as his vice president. (Harrison was the hero of the battle of Tippecanoe in 1811, when he won a victory over the Indian leader, Tecumseh.) During the 1852 election Henry Clay – who had been the party's figurehead since 1832 – died, and the Whig candidate Winfield Scott lost to Franklin Pierce. The Whigs subsequently faded from American politics, but their name and spirit lived on in such historic quilt designs as Whig Rose, Tippecanoe and Tyler Too, Clay's Choice and Whig's Defeat, shown on this page and overleaf.

This intricate patchwork and appliqué quilt is the focus of attention in a simply decorated country bedroom in Atlanta, Georgia, America. It was reportedly made by the mother of Ora Minnie Lumpkin in Floyd County, Georgia around 1856. The antique bed that the quilt covers is a traditional cannonball design. Its construction is the origin of the phrase "Night, night, sleep tight" because the mattress rests on ropes which are tightened by turning pegs. Courtesy of the Atlanta Historical Society, Inc.

Patchwork Designs

Ability level: Experienced

Size

Block: 45.7 cm/18 in square; 12 pieced
blocks and 6 plain blocks
required
Finished Quilt: 204.4 × 264 cm/80½
× 104 in

Materials

13 m/yds white fabric (includes fabric
for back of quilt)

4¼ m/yds red fabric (includes fabric
for binding)

2 m/yds green fabric

205.7 × 265.4 cm/81 × 104½ in piece
of wadding/batting (includes seam
allowance)

Template for J: 47 × 47 cm/18½ ×
18½ in sq (includes seam allowance)

Quilt Plan

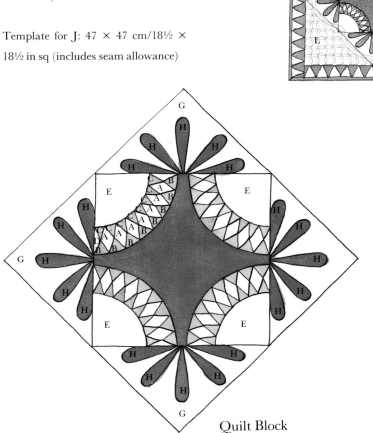

Quilt Block

Cutting

Note: A 6mm/¼ inch seam allowance
is included in all measurements; pattern pieces do not include allowance.
Quilt Back: 2 pieces, 103.5 × 265.4
cm/40¾ × 104½ in, white fabric.
Plain Blocks: 6 J squares, white fabric.
Side Triangles For side K triangles, cut
two 68 cm/26¾ in squares from white
fabric; cut each square diagonally into
4 to make 8 side triangles. Use one as
a pattern to cut 2 additional triangles.
Corner Triangles For corner L triangles,
cut two 35 cm/13⅜ in squares from
white fabric; cut in half diagonally to
make 4 corner triangles.
Borders: 158 white M triangles; 154
red M triangles; 4 red N triangles; 4
reversed red N triangles.

Binding: Cut ⅜ m/yd of red fabric
into nine 4 cm/1½ in wide strips and
sew together to measure 10⅜ m/yds.
Pattern Pieces: (Number of pieces for
one block in parenthesis. Patterns are
on pp.143 & 154-5.) A: (28) 336
white; B: (32) 384 green; C: (32) 384
green; D: (4) 48 white; D reversed: (4)
48 white; E: (4) 48 white; F: (1) 12
red; G: (4) 48 white; H: (25) 300 red.

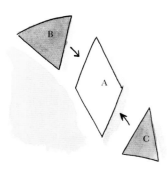

Piecing a Whig's Defeat Block

1 Sew a B and a C to each side of A to form a diagonal strip, matching notches and circles. Make six more strips for a total of seven diagonal strips.

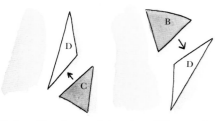

2 Sew C to lower right edge of D; match notches. Sew B to upper left of reversed D; match circles.

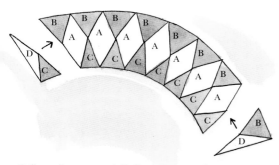

3 Sew the seven A-B-C strips together, insetting where the seams meet, to form a curved strip. Sew C-D to the left edge of the strip and B-D to the right edge of the strip. See page 129 for instructions on How to Inset.

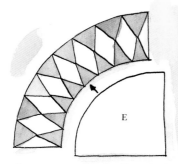

4 To make a corner unit, sew E to the inner curved edge of the pieced strip, matching the dots on E to the second and sixth A-C seams. See p. 129 for How to Sew Curves. Construct three more corner units.

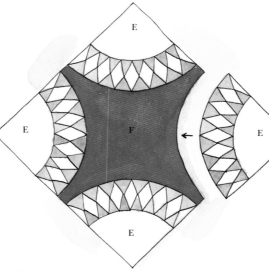

5 Sew units to F, matching X's to 2nd and 6th A-B seams.

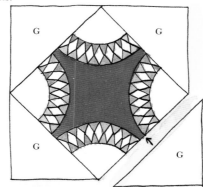

6 Sew a G to each edge of the patchwork.

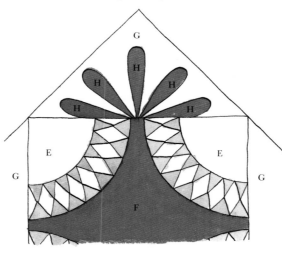

7 Prepare 25 H pieces for appliqué as directed on p. 129. Appliqué 5 H pieces to each of the G triangles.

8 Construct 11 more Whig's Defeat blocks.

Assembling and Finishing the Quilt

9 Following the Quilt Plan and working on a large flat surface, arrange the patchwork blocks with the plain J blocks to form a checkerboard. Fill in sides and corners with side K and corner L triangles.

10 The quilt is constructed in diagonal rows. Stitch blocks together in rows, working out from the middle. Sew a K or an L triangle to each end of each row.

11 Stitch rows together, matching seams carefully.

12 Next, following the Quilt Plan, construct the pieced border using the M and N triangles. For the short top and bottom edges of the quilt, sew 32 red and 33 white M triangles together, alternating colours and beginning and ending with a white M triangle. Sew an N triangle to each end of each strip. Sew the pieced borders to the top and bottom edges of quilt with red triangles innermost.

13 For the side edges of the quilt, sew 45 red and 46 white M triangles together. Sew an N triangle to each end, then sew the borders to the side edges with the red triangles innermost.

14 To make quilt back, sew the two halves together along long edges; press allowance to one side.

15 Assemble the quilt top, batting/wadding and back as directed on p. 130.

16 Outline quilt A, F and H pieces on each block.

17 Following the quilt lines shown on the Quilt Plan, work a double row of stitches around each block, curving the stitching gently to encircle the block as shown.

18 Using the quilting pattern on p. 143, fill in the background (the J, K and L pieces).

19 Bind the quilt as directed on p. 131.

Crown
of Thorns

As America was colonized, the endurance of hardship was a fact of life that turned many people to religion. And what better way was there to celebrate their faith than through the creation of a quilt based on a religious symbol?

The Bible provided inspiration for hundreds of quilt designs. The Old Testament has spawned such pattern names as David and Goliath, Joseph's Coat, Children of Israel, Solomon's Puzzle, Job's Tears and King David's Crown. New Testament patterns tended to glorify the life of Jesus Christ, with designs called Star of Bethlehem, Hosanna, Crown of Thorns and Cross and Crown. Some patterns, like Crown of Thorns, were exceedingly difficult to make and were not commonplace. But designs like Jacob's Ladder and Star and Cross were so simple that they were widely used to make everyday bedcoverings.

The Crown of Thorns quilt draped on the deck railing (left) is impressive in its intricacy. It was made in Troup County, Georgia around 1850 by Susanna Fisk McCallay. The spikey appearance of the pieces comprising the Crown of Thorns block is reminiscent of the crown made out of thorns that was placed on Jesus Christ's head after Pilate released him to the soldiers to be crucified.

The Shoo Fly quilt draped on the rocking chair was made in Knoxville, Tennessee in 1890. It was previously owned by a bag lady who lived on the streets of Knoxville. She was arrested for shoplifting and put in Mental Institution, where she died. Afterward, $10,000 and this quilt were found among her belongings. The Crown of Thorns quilt draped on the deck railing is an unusual variation; the design is also known as New York Beauty.

Patchwork Designs

Ability level: Very Experienced

Size

Block: 83.8 cm/33 in square; 6 blocks required
Finished Quilt: 218.4 × 261.6 cm/86 × 103 in

Materials

12⅜ m/yds white fabric (includes fabric for back of quilt)

4½ m/yds gold fabric (includes fabric for binding)

3⅜ m/yds of green fabric

¾ m/yd brown fabric

219.7 × 262.8 cm/86½ × 103½ in piece of wadding/batting (includes seam allowance)

Templates: N: 19 × 19 cm/7½ × 7½ in square; LL: 12.7 cm/5 in diameter circle (make out of thin cardboard).

Quilt Plan

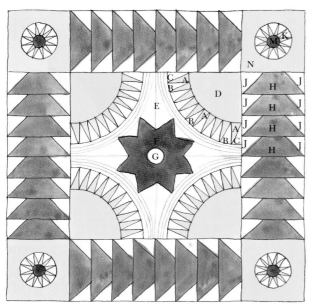

Quilt Block

Cutting

Note: A 6 mm/¼ in seam allowance is included in all measurements; pattern pieces do not include a seam allowance.

Quilt Back: 2 pieces, 110.4 × 262.8 cm/43½ × 103½ in, white fabric
Sashing: 9 O strips 6.3 × 85 cm/2½ × 33½ in, white fabric; 2 P strips 6.3 × 219.7 cm/2½ × 86½ in, white fabric
Binding: Cut nine 4 cm/1½ in wide strips across the full width of the gold fabric; stitch strips together so binding measures 10½ m/yds long.

Pattern pieces: (Number of pieces for a single block are in parenthesis. Pattern pieces are on p. 156-157.) A: (40) 240 gold; B: (36) 216 white; C: (4) 24 white; C: reversed (4) 24 white; D: (4) 24 gold; E: (1) 6 white; F: (1) 6 brown; G: (1) 6 white; H: (32) 192 green; J: (64) 384 white; K: (48) 288 gold; L (48) 288 white; M: (4) 24 brown; N: (4) 24 gold.

Side borders (make 6) H: 48 green; J: 96 white; K: 144 gold: L: 144 white; M: 12 brown; N: 12 gold.

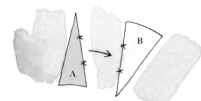

Piecing a Crown of Thorns Block

1 Sew nine A's to left edge of nine B's, matching X's.

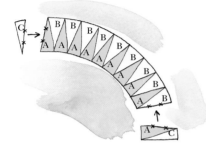

2 Sew A-B pieces together to form a curve. Sew a C to left edge of curve, matching X's. Sew an A to left edge of a reversed C, then sew to the curve matching the X's. Make three more curves.

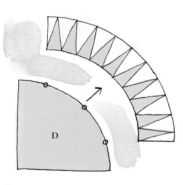

3 Sew D to one curve, matching the dots on D to the second, fifth and eighth seams of the patchwork curve. Repeat with the remaining three curves.

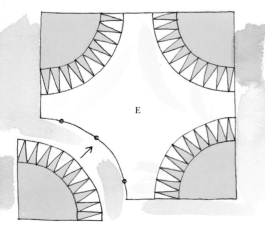

4 Sew one patchwork curve to E, matching the open circles to the second, fifth and ninth points of the curve. Fill in remaining three corners of E.

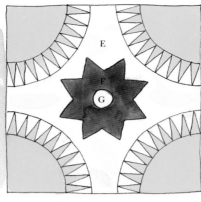

5 Prepare an F star for appliqué (see p. 129). Appliqué the star in the middle of E. Prepare a G circle for appliqué as directed on p. 113, Steps 2 and 3, making a thin cardboard template for G *without* the seam allowance. Appliqué G in middle of F star.

6 Sew a J to each angled edge of an H. Make 31 more J-H-J strips in the same manner.

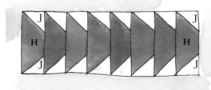

7 Sew eight J-H-J pieces together to make a border strip. Make three more border strips.

8 Sew a border strip to each side of a patchwork square, with triangles pointing in same direction on each side. Set remaining 2 border strips aside.

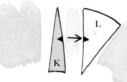

9 Construct the K-L-M roundels. Sew K to left side of L, matching notches. Repeat 11 more times.

10 Sew K-L pieces together to form a roundel; press. Prepare an M circle for appliqué as in Step 5, then appliqué over opening in middle of roundel.

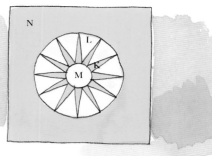

11 Using the L-L template, prepare the roundel for appliqué as in Step 5. Appliqué roundel to middle of one N square. Repeat three more times.

12 Stitch an N square to each end of the 2 border strips you set aside. Sew these to the remaining edges of the block as shown in the Block Plan with the triangles pointing in the same direction.

13 Construct five more Crown of Thorns Blocks.

Assembling and Finishing the Quilt

14 Construct six border strips as in Steps 6 and 7. Construct 12 roundels as in Steps 9 and 10. Appliqué roundels to middle of 12 N squares.

15 Arrange the blocks in 3 horizontal rows with 2 blocks in each row. Place a side border at the beginning and end of each row. Place an O sashing strip in between the blocks and side borders. Stitch together to make 3 horizontal rows.

16 Place a horizontal P sashing strip between the rows. Stitch rows to each side of P sashing strips.

17 To construct the quilt back, sew the long edges of the two fabric pieces together. Press seam to one side.

18 Assemble the layers of the quilt (see p. 130).

19 Outline-quilt A, F and G. Quilt 3 curved rows all around E; quilt straight horizontal and vertical lines across E. Outline-quilt H, K, M and edge of the roundel.

20 Bind quilt with separate binding (see p. 131).

Heavenly Stars

Quilt patterns have immortalized famous people and those who would not normally have left their mark on society. But no commemorative pattern has been so popular as that named after the two brothers who founded New Orleans in 1718. Jean Baptiste and Pierre Le Moyne were honoured by the Le Moyne Star, subsequently changed to Lemoyne Star and then corrupted in New England to Lemon Star. It is the foundation for countless designs, including the pattern seen here; the central star in isolation is a Lemoyne Star.

The Sugar Loaf quilt on the sofa was made in Gate City, Virginia by Darthula S. Wood around 1880. Below is a detail of the Heavenly Stars quilt; it was made in Tennessee around 1880.

Patchwork Designs

Ability level : Very Experienced

Size

Units: 45.7 cm/18 in square; 20 units required

Finished Quilt: 182.8 × 228.6 cm/72 × 90 in

Materials

6 m/yds white fabric (includes fabric for back of quilt and self-binding)

1¼ m/yds dark fabric

2 m/yds light fabric

1⅜ m/yds dotted fabric

¾ m/yd bright fabric

¾ m/yds striped fabric

184 × 229.8 cm/72½ × 90½ in piece of wadding/batting

Quilt Plan

Quilt Unit

Cutting

Note: All measurements include a 6 mm/¼ in seam allowance; patterns do not include seam allowance.

Quilt Back: 2 pieces, 94 × 232.4 cm/37 × 91½ in, white fabric.

Pattern Pieces: (Number of pieces for a single unit are in parenthesis. Patterns for tracing off are given on p. 155.) A: (4) 80 light; A: (4) 80 dark; A (8) 160 striped; B: (8) 160 white; C: (32) 640 light; C: (16) 320 bright; C: (16) 320 dark.

Pieces for Joining the Units: B: 66 dotted; D: 36 dotted; E: 43 dotted; F: 32 dotted.

Piecing a Heavenly Stars Unit

Note: This quilt is not constructed in blocks, but in interlinked units. The Quilt Plan on the facing page shows the position of the inner linking pieces (B, E) and the pieces used to fill in the outer edges (B, D, F).

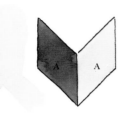

1 Sew each light A to a dark A to form a pair of diamonds.

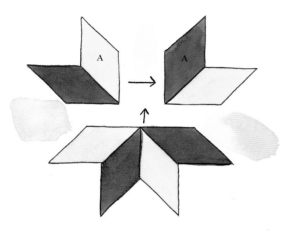

2 Sew two pairs of diamonds together to form half the central star; press the seam allowances toward the dark diamonds. Then sew the two halves together as shown to complete the star matching the seams carefully in the middle.

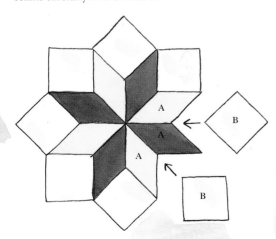

3 Inset a white B square into each angle of the central star; see How to Inset on p. 129.

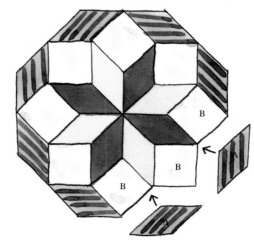

4 Inset a striped A diamond into each angle formed by the B squares.

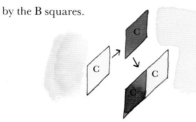

5 Next construct the pieced diamonds for the corner stars. Sew a bright C to a light C and a dark C to a light C in the order shown. Then sew the two pairs together to form a pieced C diamond. Repeat to make a total of 16 pieced C diamonds per unit.

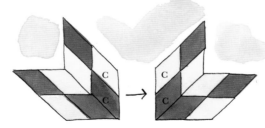

6 Sew two pieced diamonds together to form a pair, then sew two pairs together to form the corner star.

7 Sew a corner star to each diagonal A-A edge of the patchwork, matching the central seam of the star to the tip of each B square.

8 Construct 19 more Heavenly Star units.

Assembling and Finishing the Quilt

9 Following the Quilt Plan opposite and working on a large flat surface, arrange the patchwork units in five horizontal rows with four units in each row. Fill in the spaces with the remaining B, D, E and F pieces to form the quilt top.

10 To assemble the quilt top, first inset the D triangles into the C diamonds all around the outer edges of the quilt. Then inset a B square into each of the four corners of the quilt.

11 Next, inset the B squares into the C diamonds in the central portion of the quilt; see the Quilt Plan.

12 Inset the large E squares into the spaces between the units as shown in the Quilt Plan. Finally, inset the F pieces between the C diamonds around the outer edges of the quilt top.

13 To construct the quilt back, sew the two fabric pieces together along the long edges. Press the seam allowance to one side.

14 Assemble the quilt top, wadding/batting and back as directed on p. 130.

15 Quilt a diamond within each A and C diamond following the quilting lines on the patterns. Quilt an × across each B square, from corner to corner as shown on the pattern.

16 Quilt diagonal lines across the E and F pieces following the lines on the patterns.

17 Following the directions on p. 131 for a self binding, wrap the fabric from the back onto the quilt top and bind off neatly, mitring the corners.

Pine Burr

Hundreds of quilt designs made in the second half of the 19th century celebrated the natural aspects of a rapidly expanding America. Floral designs such as Rambling Rose, Meadow Daisy, Sunflower and Prairie Lily applauded the wild beauty growing all around. The plentiful foods grown on the farms were preserved through patterns called Corn and Beans, Melon Patch, Garden Basket and Fruitful Vine. And America's forests were commemorated through such designs as Maple Leaf, Forest Path, Oak Leaf and Acorn, Pine Tree and Pine Burr.

The Pine Burr quilt on the wall (see p. 139 for hanging instructions) glows with colour, although the sparkle is provided by the white triangles surrounding each patchwork unit. It has been simply quilted with diagonal parallel lines which don't detract from the intricate piecing.

This quilt was made from fabric scraps, which is why each block is pieced in a different colour combination. You can make each Pine Burr unit from a random selection of scraps if you want to achieve a similar effect. As an alternative, the instructions that follow overleaf give the required yardage for making a red, white and blue Pine Burr quilt; the blocks will resemble the central block in the quilt, just above the headboard of the bed in the photograph opposite.

Probably made in Pennsylvania, the Ocean Waves quilt on the bed dates from around 1890. It is a two-sided quilt; the other side has an Ocean Waves pattern in the same fabrics, but in miniature scale. What is even more amazing about this quilt is that there is another quilt inside! Because of its thickness, the quilt was tied.

The String Star quilt on the chair back was made in Kentucky around 1917, while the Flagstones quilt folded on the blanket chest at the foot of the bed was made by Drucilla Badgett in Knoxville, Tennessee around 1906. It was her first quilt but she never liked it so it wasn't used. The 1880s Pine Burr quilt (described above) is from Tennessee.

Patchwork Designs

Ability Level: Very experienced

Size

Unit: 31.7 × 31.7 cm/12½ × 12½ in;
12 units required

Finished Quilt: 123.1 × 154.9 cm/48½ × 61 in

Materials

4⅝ m/yds navy blue fabric (includes fabric for borders and back of quilt)

1½ m/yds royal blue fabric

½ m/yd red fabric

1⅛ m/yds white fabric (includes fabric for binding)

124.4 × 156.2 cm/49 × 61½ in piece of wadding/batting (includes seam allowance)

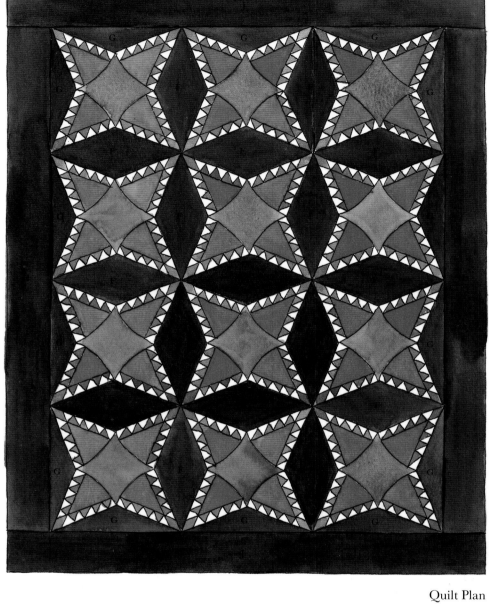

Quilt Plan

Quilt Unit

Cutting

Note: A 6 mm/¼ in seam allowance is included in all measurements; pattern pieces do not include a seam allowance.

Quilt Back: 2 pieces, 62.8 × 156.2 cm/ 24¾ × 61½ in, navy blue fabric.

Borders: 2 H strips 15.2 × 128.2 cm/6 × 50½ in, navy blue; 2 J strips 15.2 × 124.4 cm/6 × 49 in, navy blue.

Binding: Cut five 4 cm/1½ in wide strips across the full width of the white fabric. Then stitch these five strips together so that the binding measures 6 m/yds long.

Pattern Pieces: (Number of pieces for a single unit are in parenthesis. Patterns are on p. 152-3.) A: (16) 192 white; A reversed: (16) 192 white; A: (16) 192 royal blue; A reversed: (16) 192 royal blue; B: (4) 48 white; B reversed: (4) 48 white; C: (4) 48 red; D: (4) 48 royal blue; E: (1) 12 royal blue; F: 17 navy blue; G: 14 navy blue.

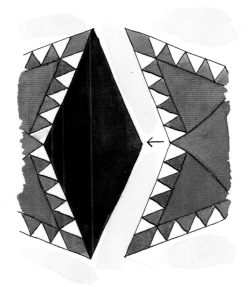

Piecing a Pine Burr Unit

Note: This quilt is not constructed in blocks, but in interlinked units.

1 Sew a white A piece to a royal blue A piece. Repeat 15 more times for a total of 16 A-A pieces.

2 Sew four A-A pieces together to make a strip, alternating the royal blue and white fabrics as shown. Sew a B piece to the royal blue A piece at the right edge of the strip. Repeat this process three more times for a total of four strips.

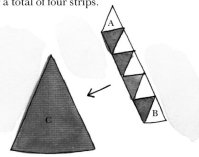

3 Sew the strips that you just made to the right edge of four C pieces.

4 Sew a reversed royal blue A piece to a reversed white A piece as shown. Repeat 15 more times for a total of 16 A-A pieces.

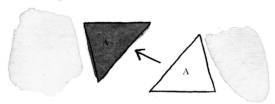

5 Sew four A-A pieces together to make a strip, alternating the royal blue and white as you did in Step 2. Sew a reversed B piece to the royal blue A

piece at the left edge of each strip. Sew a D piece to the white A piece at the right edge of each strip. Repeat this process three more times for a total of four strips.

6 Sew the strips that you made in Step 5 to the left edge of the C pieces as shown above.

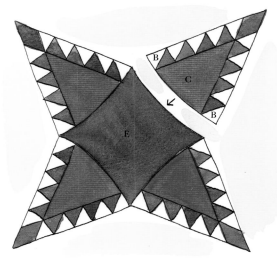

7 Sew each of the C triangles to an E piece, easing the fabrics together carefully along the curved edges (see How to Sew Curves on p. 129). Gently press each curve after sewing.

8 Construct 11 more Pine Burr Variation Units in the same manner.

Assembling the Quilt

9 Following the Quilt Plan on the opposite page and working on a large flat surface, arrange the patch-work units in four horizontal rows with three units in each row. Fill in the spaces between the units with the F diamonds. Fill in the outer edges of the patchwork with the G half-diamonds.

10 Inset the F diamonds in a vertical position between the patchwork units to join them into horizontal rows (see How to Inset on p. 129).

11 Inset the F diamonds in a horizontal position between the rows to join the rows together. Take extra care at the tips of each unit, as these areas will be tricky to piece.

12 Inset the G half-diamonds into the units all around the edges of the patchwork.

13 Stitch the H border strips to each side of the patchwork.

14 Finally, stitch the J border strips to the top and bottom of the patchwork to complete the quilt top.

15 To construct the quilt back, sew the two fabric pieces together along the long edges. Press the seam allowance to one side.

16 Assemble the quilt top, wadding/batting and back as directed on p. 130.

Finishing the Quilt

17 Quilt the entire design with straight parallel diagonal lines, spaced 1.9 cm/¾ in apart.

18 Bind the quilt with a separate binding as directed on p. 131.

Berta Larsson Quilt

Sweden has a quilting tradition that dates back to the middle of the 18th century. Colourful patchwork quilts have been constructed from the scraps left over from making everyday clothing; a woman would wait until she had saved enough scraps before beginning to make a quilt. The Log Cabin seems to have been the pattern most favoured by Swedish quilters, but other motifs have been used including stars, honeycombs and triangles as well as original designs.

The unusual patchwork quilt shown on the left was made by Berta Larsson, who was born in 1911 in Långgården outside Vara in Sweden. She was the eldest daughter of a farming family and had nine brothers and sisters. Berta learned how to sew and specialized in making women's coats. During the 1930s, she began to make quilts from the leftover scraps of cotton sateen coat linings. She quilted her work entirely by hand on a frame made by her father. Berta Larsson died at the age of 39, but left the wonderful legacy of her quilts, which are now being exhibited all over Sweden in an exhibition entitled *Lapptäcken-en kulturskatt* – "A Cultural Treasury of Patchwork Quilts", produced by Åsa Wettre.

The 1930s Berta Larsson Quilt was photographed at the Mölndals Museum near Gothenburg, Sweden. The Mölndals Museum focuses on the everyday lives of the Swedish people and features traditional furniture, accessories and textiles in authentic room settings. The quilt will be featured in "Old Swedish Quilts" by Åsa Wettre (see the Directory).

Patchwork Designs

Ability Level: Intermediate

Size

Block: 30.4 cm/12 in square; 15 blocks
Finished Quilt: 152.4 × 213.3 cm/60 × 84 in

Materials

6⅛ m/yds gold fabric (includes borders, back and self-binding)

⅝ m/yd rust fabric

½ m/yd brown fabric

½ m/yd green fabric

½ m/yd cream fabric

153.6 × 214.6 cm/60½ × 84½ in piece of wadding/batting

Templates for: A: 8.8 cm/3½ in square; B: 5 × 20.3 cm/2 × 8 in rectangle (both include seam allowance)

Quilt Plan

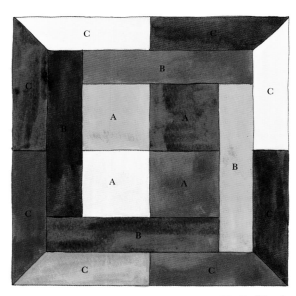

Quilt Block

Cutting

Note: A 6mm/¼ inch seam allowance is included; pattern pieces do not include a seam allowance.
Quilt Back: 2 pieces, 107.9 × 153.6 cm/ 42½ × 60½ in, gold fabric
Borders: 2 D strips 31/7 × 92.7 cm/ 12½ × 36½ in, gold fabric; 2 E strips 31.7 × 214.6 cm/12½ × 84½ in, gold fabric

Pattern Pieces: (Number of pieces for a single block in parenthesis; see Step 1 for ways to cut A pieces.)
A: (1) 15 cream; A: (1) 15 gold; A: (1) 15 green; A: (1) 15 rust; B (1) 15 gold; B (1) 15 green; B: (1) 15 rust; B: (1) 15 brown; C: (2) 30 cream; C: (2) 30 rust; C reversed: (2) 30 brown; C reversed: (1) 15 gold; C reversed: (1) 15 green

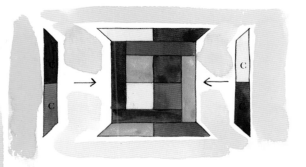

Piecing a Patchwork Block

1 To make the middle of the block use templates or rotary cutting. With templates, sew each cream A to a gold A square, making 15 pieced rectangles. Sew each rust A to a green A, making 15 rectangles. Sew rectangles together to make central square.

2 From the full width of the fabric, cut two strips each from the cream, gold, rust and green fabrics, making each strip 8.8 cm/3½ in wide.

3 Sew gold strips to cream strips; press seam allowances toward gold fabric. Measure 8.8 cm/3½ in away from end of pressed strips and cut to form a pieced rectangle. Cut 14 more pieced rectangles.

4 Sew green strips to rust strips; press seam allowances toward rust fabric. Measure 8.8 cm/3½ in away from end of pressed strips and cut to form a pieced rectangle. Cut 14 more pieced rectangles.

5 Sew gold/cream to green/rust rectangles as shown in Step 1, matching seam allowances.

6 With right sides facing, position a green B strip over patchwork, matching right edges and allowing left edge of B to extend beyond patchwork. Stitch together from middle of seam toward edges.

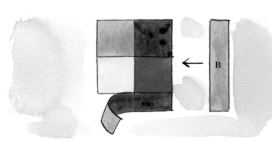

7 Stitch a gold B to right edge of patchwork; press.

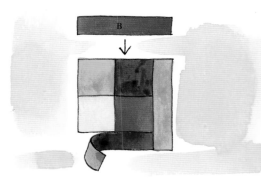

8 Stitch a rust B to top edge of patchwork; press.

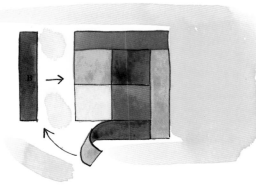

9 Stitch a brown B to left edge of patchwork; press.

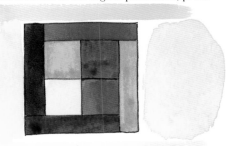

10 Sew remainder of seam of first B strip to complete central portion of patchwork. Press.

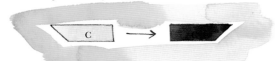

11 Sew each cream C to a reversed brown C. Sew each rust C to a reversed gold or green C.

12 Sew C-C strips to top and bottom of patchwork. Sew remaining C-C strips to sides. Mitre corners.

13 Construct 14 more patchwork blocks.

Assembly and Finishing

14 Following the Quilt Plan and working on a large flat surface, arrange the patchwork blocks in 5 horizontal rows with 3 blocks in each row.

15 Stitch blocks together in rows, then stitch rows together, matching seams at intersections.

16 Stitch a D border strip to the top and bottom edges of the patchwork and an E border strip to each side to complete the quilt top.

17 For quilt back, sew two fabric pieces together along long edges. Press seam allowance to one side.

18 Assemble the quilt (see page 130).

19 Outline-quilt the squares in the middle of each patchwork block.

20 Outline-quilt inner and outer edges of B strips; inner and outer edges of C strips, as well as the mitred seams in each corner.

21 Following the Quilt Plan, measure and mark three quilting lines around the borders. The first line should be 7.6 cm cm/3 in away from the edge of the patchwork, the second 15.2 cm/6in away and the third 22.8 cm/9 in away. Quilt borders along marked lines.

22 Fold raw edges of quilt top and back 6mm/¼ in *inside* quilt, enclosing all raw edges and wadding/batting. Slipstitch edges together invisibly.

Spinning Stars

The most popular single image in the quilting world is the star. Hundreds of different star designs have been developed, changed, copied and improved upon over the years. Stars can be pieced, appliquéd or quilted in numerous configurations. The star itself can have five, six or eight points, and some "star" designs do not actually look like stars at all!

Probably the most popular star and the easiest to construct is called Ohio Star. This design is composed of a single large square surrounded by eight triangular points; see the photograph on p. 140. The Variable Star is an adaptation of this, with the central square turned on point in order to give the design added dimension. The Lemoyne Star, discussed on p. 82 and composed of diamonds, is the basis for literally hundreds of other star designs. The Lone Star or Star of Bethlehem (see p. 28) is one of the most dramatic quilt designs. Its huge central star blazes with colour and is usually set against a dark background. It is often surrounded by intricate appliqué or quilting.

This Spinning Stars quilt is a rare pattern, and one that seems to vibrate with movement. It was made from fabric scraps, which is why each block is different. You can make each Spinning Stars block from random scraps in order to achieve a similar effect. Alternatively, the instructions that follow give the required yardage for making a white, orange and blue quilt; the finished piece will resemble the Quilt Plan illustration overleaf.

Gossamer curtains and rough wooden walls are the perfect backdrop for this Spinning Stars scrap quilt, made in Texas around 1840. It is resting on a wooden bed next to a simple rush chair.

Patchwork Designs

Ability Level : Experienced

Size

Block: 30.4 cm/12 in square; 42 blocks required

Finished Quilt: 182.8 × 213.3 cm/72 × 84 in

Materials

8½ m/yds light fabric (includes fabric for back of quilt)

3 m/yds striped fabric

3⅛ m/yds dark fabric (includes fabric for binding)

184.1 × 214.6 cm/72½ × 84½ in piece of wadding/batting (includes seam allowance)

Quilt Plan

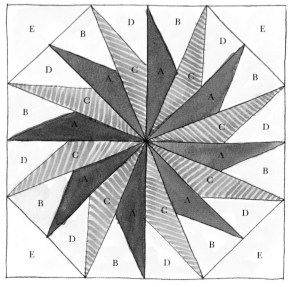

Quilt Block

Cutting

Note: A 6 mm/¼ in seam allowance is included in all measurements; pattern pieces do not include a seam allowance.

Quilt Back: 2 pieces, 107.9 × 184.1 cm/42½ × 72½ in light fabric.

Binding: Cut seven 4 cm/1½ in wide strips across the full width of the dark fabric, and one 4 cm/1½ in wide strip across half the width; stitch strips together so binding measures 9 m/yds long.

Pattern Pieces: (Number of pieces for a single block are in parenthesis. Patterns are on p. 153.) A: (8) 336 dark; B: (8) 336 light; C: (8) 336 striped; D: (8) 336 light; E: (4) 168 light.

Note: If you cut the pattern pieces as directed above, you will create a very dramatic quilt. If you feel the design is too graphic for your bed, you can tone down the quilt by inserting a plain block in between each patchwork block.

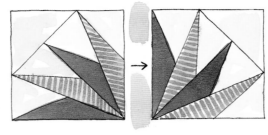

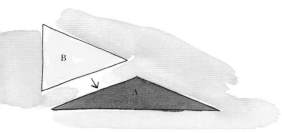

Piecing a Spinning Stars Block

1 Sew a B to the left diagonal edge of A. Repeat 7 more times for a total of 8 A-B pieces.

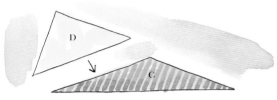

2 Sew a D to the left diagonal edge of C. Repeat 7 more times for a total of 8 C-D pieces.

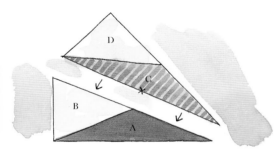

3 Sew a C-D to an A-B piece matching the X on C to the A-B seam. Repeat 7 more times for a total of 8 pairs.

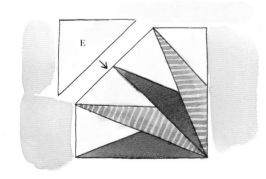

4 Sew 2 of the pairs just made together matching the dot on A to the C-D seam. Then, sew an E triangle to the angled edge as shown to complete one quarter of the block.

5 Construct three more quarters in the same manner being sure to position the colours exactly the same for each quarter.

6 Sew two quarters together for one half of the block. Repeat this process with the other two quarters in order to make the other half of the block.

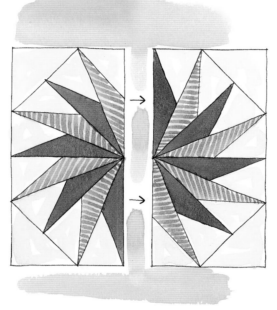

7 Next sew the two halves of the blocks together. With the right sides together, align the exact middles of the two halves, fanning the seam allowances to make the central portion feel quite flat. In order to match the seams perfectly in the middle, it is most important that the *centre* seam allowances go in opposite directions. Look at the wrong side of the patchwork and note that the stitched seams form a "V" shape in the middle. Insert the point of a pin through the bottom of the V on the wrong side of one half, making sure that the pin comes out at the tip of a point on the right side. Then insert the point of the same pin through the tip of the matching point on the other half, making sure that it comes out at the bottom of the V on the wrong side of the other half. Carefully adjust the two pieces so that they align on the pin, then secure the join by pinning to the right and left side of the central point.

8 Sew the halves together to complete the block, making sure that you stitch precisely across the bottom of the V. Make sure that you remove the pins before sewing over them or you may run the risk of breaking your sewing machine needle as the many layers will make the central area quite thick.

9 Construct 41 more Spinning Stars Blocks in the same manner.

Assembling the Quilt

10 Following the Quilt Plan on the opposite page and working on a large flat surface, arrange the patchwork blocks in seven horizontal rows with six blocks in each row.

11 Sew the blocks together in rows, carefully matching edges of the E triangles and the points of the stars where they meet.

12 Sew the rows together, matching the seams carefully at the intersections and again matching the edges of the E triangles and the points of the stars where they meet.

13 To construct the quilt back, sew the two fabric pieces together along the long edges. Press the seam allowance to one side.

14 Assemble the quilt top, wadding/batting and back as directed on p. 130.

Finishing the Quilt

15 Outline-quilt the A and C pieces; do not work a double line of quilting where the pieces meet.

16 Quilt 6 mm/¼ in away from the seam allowances around the outer edge of each block and the diagonal edges of the E triangles as shown in the photograph. Or for contrast, quilt a circle within the square formed by the junction of 4 E triangles.

17 Bind the quilt with a separate binding as directed on p. 131.

Appliqué Designs

Appliqué has always been the decorative member of the quilting family; from heraldic banners and ecclesiastical robes to magnificent Baltimore Album quilts, this technique is ornamental and work-intensive.

Appliqué can be done on the sewing machine, but the results would not be like those you see in this book. Most of these quilts were appliquéd by hand, and the soft, subtle roundness of the pieces would be compromised by stitching them on a machine, therefore directions for machine-appliqué have not been included in this book.

If you decide to make an appliqué quilt, first read the instructions and study the illustrations for How to Appliqué on p. 129, then read the hints that follow.

Choose your fabrics with care – if you are cutting out a flower or a leaf, see if you can find a naturalistic print to make the finished effect more realistic. Unless you want to make a bold statement, do not use large or geometric prints which would take away from the softness of the designs. When marking the appliqués on the right side of the fabric, position the pieces so that the curves are on the bias; this will make it easier to achieve a smooth finish. After a block has been appliquéd, press it from the wrong side on a fluffy towel so that the appliqués are not compressed, which could cause the seam allowances to show through. When pressing from the wrong side, smooth a white handkerchief over the appliquéd area so that the iron does not catch the threads.

The North Carolina Lily quilt shown here boasts both appliqué and patchwork in its construction. Simple lozenge quilting brings the sashing and borders to life. It was probably made in Illinois around 1880.

Rose
Wreath

Up until the 1850s and 1860s, the women who lived along the East coast of America were leading comparable lives, with similar aspirations and experiences. They had the same sources for their fabrics and design ideas, and the quilts they made were, on the whole, quite homogeneous. But once families started moving West, the differences between those in the East and those who took the pioneer trail grew.

The pioneer women were reduced to circumstances akin to those that the early settlers of America had experienced. Once they had settled into their homes – if indeed, they survived the journey at all – these plucky women made mostly utilitarian patchwork quilts. Designs such as Prairie Queen, Rocky Road to Kansas, Trail of the Covered Wagon, Bear's Paw, Indian Hatchet and Road to California were evocative of the new sights and circumstances they were encountering.

At the same time, women living on the East Coast became enamoured of dressing well and decorating their homes beautifully. Intricate appliquéd quilts requiring hours of time were made during this period, including designs like Princess Feather, Star and Plume and Garden Maze.

Floral quilts, particularly in shades of red, green and white, were very popular during the 1850s and 1860s. Classical designs such as wreaths and flowers in urns became fashionable. So the combination of a rose and a wreath in one design was hard to resist.

The 19th-century Rose Wreath quilt on the simple wooden bed was used as a summer counterpane and was backed but not quilted. The instructions that follow are for a padded quilt that is outline-quilted around the appliqués.

Appliqué Designs

Ability Level : Intermediate

Size

Block: 40.6 cm/16 in square; 20 blocks required

Finished Quilt: 203.2 × 243.8 cm/80 × 96 in

Materials

13 m/yds white fabric (includes fabric for back of quilt; see note on cutting this fabric under *Borders* below)

5 m/yds green fabric (includes fabric for binding)

1¼ m/yds red fabric

204.4 × 245.1 cm/80½ × 96½ in piece of wadding/batting (includes seam allowance)

Template for C: 41.9 cm/16½ in square (background block; includes seam allowance)

Quilt Plan

Quilt Block

Cutting

Note: A 6 mm/¼ in seam allowance is included in all measurements; patterns do not include a seam allowance.

Quilt Back: 2 pieces, 102.8 × 245.1 cm/40½ × 96½ in, white fabric.

Borders: 2 F strips 21.5 × 204.4 cm/ 8½ × 80½ in, white fabric; 2 G strips 21.5 × 245.1 cm/8½ × 96½ in, white fabric. Note: To conserve white fabric, cut single G strip along left edge, and 10 C squares next to it. Repeat, then cut F strips from remaining fabric.

Blocks: 20 C squares, white fabric.

Bias Strip for Vines: From green fabric,

cut two 111.7 cm/44 in squares and one 7.6 cm/3 in square. Following instructions for bias binding on p. 130, cut 2.54 cm/1 in wide strips and sew to measure 26½m/yds long.

Binding: Cut eight 4 cm/1½ in wide strips across the full width of green fabric; stitch together so binding measures 10 m/yds long.

Pattern Pieces: (Number of pieces for a single block are in parenthesis. Patterns are on p. 152.) A: (4) 80 red; B: (20) 400 green. Border: A: 18 red; B: 36 green; D: 22 red; E: 44 green.

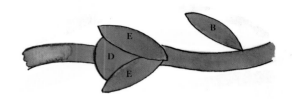

Piecing a Rose Wreath Block

1 Find the exact middle of a C square by folding and pressing the square in half horizontally and then vertically. Using a compass, mark a 26.6 cm/10½ in diameter circle in the middle of the fabric.

2 Cut an 82.5 cm/32½ in length of the green bias strip for the vine. Press both long edges of the vine 6 mm/¼ in to the wrong side; the finished width of the vine will be 13 mm/½ in.

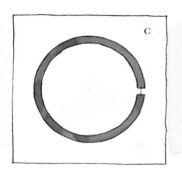

3 Beginning in the middle of one side edge of the block, centre the pressed vine over the marked line on the background. (A flower will cover the beginning and end of the vine, so you do not have to finish off the edges, nor do the edges need to meet.) Pin and baste the vine in place, using a steam iron to remove any pleats or puckers so the vine forms a smooth curve. After the vine has been basted, appliqué it to the background fabric as directed on p. 129.

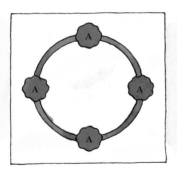

4 Prepare four flowers for appliqué as directed on p. 129. Position each flower on the vine as shown. Pin, baste and then appliqué each flower in place.

5 Prepare 20 leaves for appliqué as directed in Appliqued Leaves on p. 107. Following the Quilt Block illustration, pin outer leaves between each flower. Then pin two inner leaves between each flower. Baste, then appliqué in place.

6 Construct 19 more Rose Wreath Blocks.

Appliquéd Borders

7 Appliqué borders before sewing to quilt top. Zigzag-stitch the edges to keep them from fraying.

8 Fold each border in half crosswise to find the centre point; mark with a pin. Fold each border in half lengthwise and press; the pressed crease will be your guide for positioning the vine.

9 Mark a dot on the pressed crease at the centre point; remove the pin. Measure and mark dots at 20.3 cm/8 in intervals to the left and right of centre. On the F borders, mark 4 dots to the left and right of centre. On the G borders, mark 5 dots to the left and right of centre. These dots indicate the placement of roses and buds.

10 Cut bias vine into two 172.7 cm/68 in pieces for F borders, and two 210.8 cm/83 in pieces for G borders. Prepare vines as directed in Step 2.

11 Following the Quilt Plan and using the marked dots as a guide, pin one vine to the F border, making 8 gentle curves. Note that the vine curves *between* the dots. Cut away any excess vine at the end. Baste the vine to the border, then press so that the curves are smooth with no puckers. Appliqué the vine to the border. Repeat for the other F border.

12 For the G border, pin the vine to G making 10 curves as shown on the Quilt Plan. Trim away any excess vine. Baste, press and appliqué the vine as you did for F. Repeat for other G border.

13 Prepare the remaining pieces for appliqué. Do not turn the bottom edge of the D bud under where it will be hidden beneath the E leaves (marked with X's on the pattern).

14 Following the Quilt Plan, position the leaves, flowers and buds on the borders, pinning them in place over the previously marked dots. Once you are satisfied with their position, appliqué the flowers, leaves and buds to the borders. To construct the buds, overlap D with the two E leaves.

Assembling and Finishing the Quilt

15 Following the Quilt Plan and working on a large flat surface, arrange the appliquéd blocks in five horizontal rows, with four blocks in each row.

16 Stitch the blocks together in rows, then stitch the rows together, matching the seams carefully at the intersections.

17 Sew an F border to the top and bottom of the appliquéd middle, allowing the ends of the borders to extend beyond the top for mitring.

18 Stitch G borders to sides of quilt top, allowing ends to extend beyond the top for mitring.

19 Mitre the corners of the borders following the directions on p. 130.

20 To construct the quilt back, sew the two fabric pieces together along the long edges. Press the seam allowance to one side.

21 Assemble the quilt top, wadding/batting and back as directed on p. 130.

22 Outline-quilt the vine, flowers and leaves on each block and the appliqués on the borders.

23 Bind the quilt with a separate binding as directed on p. 131.

Love Apple

The appliqué quilt draped on the chair in the middle of the photograph opposite is called Love Apple. A "love apple" was actually a tomato, initially grown only for ornamental purposes and never consumed because it was considered inedible. The bright red fruit appealed to gardeners as well as quilters. A good many Love Apple quilts were made, mainly in red and green colourways, with highlights of yellow, throughout the 19th century.

The beauty of this quilt lies in its simplicity. Each block has one graceful flower, which connects to the flowers in the other blocks at the base of each stem. There are two ways that you can position appliqués on the background fabric. For a precise result, which you would need for making a quilt such as this, sketch the design on the background fabric before positioning the appliqués. As an alternative, if you are going to make only one Love Apple block – perhaps for a small project like a cushion or pillow – you can assemble the appliqués on the background by eye, making any adjustments as you go.

Many old quilts are known by several different names – all equally charming. The Nile green and white Virginia Reel quilt in the foreground is also known as Snail Trail or Monkey Wrench; it was made in Missouri in the 1930s.

Draping quilts over a beam is an effective way to display extra pieces, especially if space is at a premium. The patchwork Tree of Life quilt on the left was made around 1880. The Primitive Flower quilt on the right was made in Appalachia in the 1920s; it is the only machine-appliquéd quilt in the book. The background fabric on the front and back of the Primitive Flower quilt is comprised of old feed sacks. The quilt was exhibited in the Museum of Appalachia until they closed their quilt department; it was bought at an auction. The Love Apple quilt draped on the chair (described above) was made in Iowa between 1860 and 1880.

Appliqué Designs

Ability level: Experienced

Size

Block: 33 cm/13 in square; 36 blocks required

Finished Quilt: 232.4 × 232.4 cm/91½ × 91½ in

Materials

12¼ m/yds white fabric (includes fabric for back of quilt and fold-finished edge)

3¾ m/yds green fabric

1⅜ m/yds red fabric

½ m/yd yellow fabric

232.4 × 232.4 cm/91½ × 91½ in piece of wadding/batting (includes seam allowance)

Template for Background: 34.2 × 34.2 cm/13½ × 13½ in square (includes seam allowance)

Quilt Plan

Quilt Block

Cutting

Note: A 6 mm/¼ in seam allowance is included in all measurements; patterns do not include seam allowance.

Quilt Back: One central panel, 111.7 × 233.6 cm/44 × 92 in, white fabric; 2 side panels, 62.2 × 233.6 cm/24½ × 92 in, white fabric.

Borders: Two S strips 17.7 × 199.3 cm/7 × 78½ in, white fabric; Two T strips 17.7 × 233.6 cm/7 × 92 in, white fabric.

Background Blocks: 36 squares, using the Background template.

Bias Strip for Stems and Vines: From green fabric, cut one 111.7 cm/44 in square and one 33 cm/13 in square.

Following the instructions for bias binding on p. 130, cut 2.54 cm/1 in wide bias strips and sew together to measure 16½ m/yds long.

Pattern Pieces: (Number of pieces for a single block are in parenthesis. Patterns are on pp. 158-159.) A: (1) 36 green; B: (1) 18 green; B reversed: (1) 18 green; C: (1) 36 red; D: (1) 36 yellow. Border F: 148 green; G: 4 green; G reversed: 4 green; H: 8 red; J: 8 yellow; K: 4 green; K reversed: 4 green; L: 16 green; M: 40 red; M: 16 green; N: 8 yellow; O: 6 green; O reversed: 6 green; P: 4 green; Q: 4 green; R: 4 red.

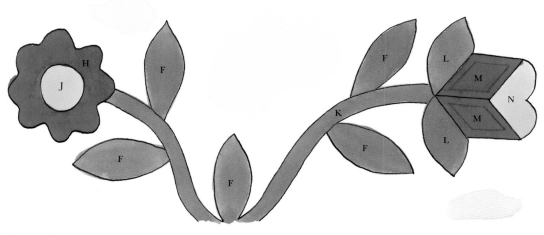

Border Plan A

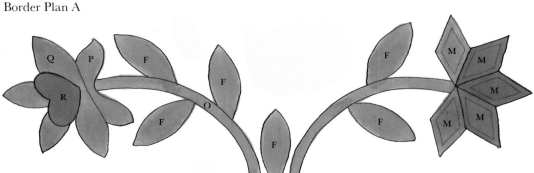

Border Plan B

Note: The border designs shown above and on the Quilt Plan, left, are only suggestions. You are free to arrange the appliqués in any way you wish. You can look at the borders for the Rose Wreath quilt illustrated on p. 102 and the Berry Block Quilt illustrated on p. 114 for other ideas.

How to Appliqué Leaves

Pointed edges, such as the tips of leaves can be tricky to appliqué. First, clip into the seam allowance 6 mm/¼ in below the point; trim the seam allowance to 3 mm/⅛ in then cut off the point 3 mm/⅛ in away from the marked turning line (far left). Fold the point to the wrong side (centre left). Fold one edge of the appliqué 6 mm/¼ in to the wrong side (centre right), then fold the second edge to the wrong side, overlapping the first edge (right). Baste the edges in place and press carefully. Don't make extra work for yourself or extra bulk beneath the appliqués; read the instructions carefully for the appliqué design you have chosen to see whether it is necessary to turn all the edges under, or whether the raw edges will be hidden beneath another appliqué.

Piecing a Love Apple Block

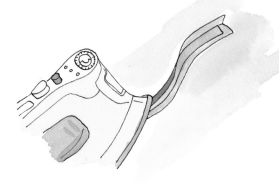

1 Prepare the A stem (and all other stems in this quilt) as follows: Trace the full-size stem pattern and make a template (without seam allowances) out of thin cardboard. For the A stem, cut a strip 26.6 cm/10½ in long out of the 2.54 cm/1 in wide bias strip. Place the bias strip, wrong side up, on your ironing board. Centre the cardboard template right side down on the bias strip; use your fingers to

adjust the bias strip to follow the contours of the template. Using a steam iron, carefully fold each long edge of the strip 6 mm/¼ in over onto the cardboard, steam-pressing the fabric in place as you go. Because the strip is cut on the bias, you should be able to follow the curves of the template without making any creases or puckers in the fabric. If the fabric does crease or pucker, just press out the area and begin again. If you work slowly and carefully you will achieve good results; also, the work will get easier as you progress. However, you may find that the steam-pressing wears out your template more quickly than ordinary use. To save time, prepare three or four cardboard templates before beginning, and discard them as they lose their shape. Do not turn the short ends of the stem under. Turn the stem over to the right side and steam-press gently, then carefully slip out the template (right).

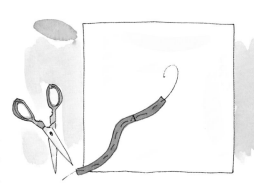

2 Prepare pieces B, B reversed, C, D and E for appliqué as directed on p. 129; also see the instructions above (under Appliquéd Leaves) for turning under the pointed edges of the B, D and E pieces. However, do not turn the straight bottom edges of the B leaves under because they will be tucked beneath the stems. Also, do not turn the bottom edge of the C flower under where it will be tucked beneath D (this area is marked with X's on the pattern).

Appliqué Designs

3 Gently place the prepared A stem on the right side of one background block. Trim off the ends of the stem that extend beyond the edges of the background. Baste the stem to the background.

4 Position the B leaves on each side of the A stem between the areas marked with dots on the pattern; tuck the unpressed ends of the leaves 6 mm/¼ in beneath the stem. Baste the leaves in place, then appliqué the stem and leaves to the background.

5 Position the C and D pieces on the background, tucking the raw edges of C beneath D. You can experiment with the placement of the C and D pieces – changing the angle slightly will give a very different appearance to the finished design. Baste in place, then appliqué the pieces to the background using matching thread.

6 Place E in the middle of C, centred between the top and bottom edges of the flower. Baste in place, then appliqué to C.

7 Construct 35 more Love Apple Blocks in the same manner.

Assembling the Quilt

8 Following the Quilt Plan and working on a large flat surface, arrange the appliquéd blocks in six rows with six blocks in each row. Position the blocks in groups of four with all the stems in a group pointing toward the middle, forming an "X" as shown in the Quilt Plan.

9 Stitch the blocks together in rows, then stitch the rows together, matching seams carefully at each intersection. The raw ends of the A stems will be enclosed in the seams; make sure that the edges of the stems match.

10 Stitch an S border to the top and bottom edges of the quilt top.

11 Stitch a T border to each side of the piece to complete the quilt top.

12 To construct the quilt back, sew a side panel to each long edge of the central panel, matching edges carefully. Press the seam allowances to one side.

Appliquéd Border

13 Prepare 14 F leaves for appliqué as directed on the previous page, turning all raw edges under.

14 Place the quilt top on a flat surface with the S border strips at the top and bottom edges. Measure and mark with a pin the following distances from the left side of the quilt along the bottom edge: 29.2 cm/11½ in, 85 cm/33½ in, 148.5 cm/58½ in and 204.4 cm/80½ in. Remove each pin and place one F leaf in its place, with the bottom edge of each leaf 1.3 cm/½ in above the raw edge; baste in place. Repeat in the same manner for the top edge.

15 Measure and mark with a pin the following distances from the left side of the quilt along one T border strip: 50.8 cm/20 in, 116.8 cm/46 in and 182.8 cm/72 in. Remove each pin and place one F leaf in its place, with the bottom edge of each leaf 1.3 cm/½ in above the raw edge; baste in place. Repeat in the same manner for the opposite side.

16 Appliqué the basted F leaves in place.

17 Make 8 J-H flowers as follows: cut 8 bias strips, each 15.2 cm/6 in long. Prepare the G and reversed G stems as directed in Step 1. Prepare the J and H pieces for appliqué. Following the Quilt Plan for position on the quilt top and Border Plan A, arrange one G stem, 3 F leaves and one H flower on the border; appliqué in place. Then appliqué J in the middle of the flower. Repeat for the other 7 J-H flowers, referring to the Quilt Plan for position.

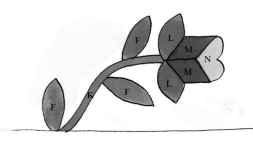

18 Make 8 M-N flowers as follows: Cut 8 bias strips, each 20.3 cm/8 in long. Prepare the K and reversed K stems as directed in Step 1. Stitch 8 pairs of red M's together for the flowers, then prepare the L, M-M and N pieces for appliqué as directed on p. 129. Do not turn the bottom edges of the N pieces under, as they will be tucked beneath the M flowers. Following the Quilt Plan for position on the quilt top and Border Plan A, arrange one K stem, 3 F leaves, 2 L leaves, one M-M flower and one N heart on the border; appliqué in place. Repeat for the other 7 M-N flowers, referring to the Quilt Plan for position.

19 Make 8 M flowers as follows: Cut 8 bias strips, each 21.5 cm/8½ in long. Prepare the O and reversed O stems as directed in Step 1. Sew 3 red M's together to form the petals; sew a green M to each side of the petals for the leaves as shown. Make 7 more M flowers/leaves in the same manner. Then prepare these pieces for appliqué. Following the Quilt Plan and Border Plan B, arrange one O stem, 3 F leaves and one M flower on the border; appliqué in place. Repeat for the other 7 M flowers referring to the Quilt Plan for position.

20 Make 4 Q-R flowers as follows: Cut 4 bias strips,

each 21.5 cm/8½ in long. Prepare the O and the reversed O stems as directed in Step 1. Prepare the P, Q and R pieces for appliqué as directed on p. 129. Do not turn the top edges of the P pieces under, as they will be tucked beneath the Q leaves. Following the Quilt Plan for position on the quilt top and Border Plan B, arrange one stem, 4 F leaves, one P leaf and one Q piece on the border; appliqué in place. Then appliqué one R heart on top of the Q piece. Repeat for the other 3 Q-R flowers, referring to the Quilt Plan for position.

Finishing the Quilt

21 Assemble the quilt top, wadding/batting and back as directed on p. 130.

22 Outline-quilt the A stem on each block. Following the quilting lines on the pattern pieces and the Block Plan, quilt the B, C, D and E pieces. If you wish, you can use quilting threads in colours to match the appliqué pieces. This would be particularly effective if the back of the quilt is a solid white fabric.

23 Outline-quilt the flowers, leaves and stems on the borders. Quilt the M pieces as shown on the pattern.

24 Using the feather quilting pattern on p. 143 as a guide, quilt the entire background of the quilt in an interwoven feather design. First, quilt a meandering feather along the seams, adjusting the pattern where the feathers cross horizontally and vertically. Then add quilting in between the flowers and leaves on the blocks and borders. Add as little or as much feather quilting as you wish. Alternatively, you can quilt the background with horizontal and vertical lines, spaced about 2 cm/¾ in apart. Do not let your quilting stitches go within 2.54 cm/1 in of the edge of the quilt.

25 When the quilting is done, fold the raw edges of the quilt top and back 1.3 cm/½ in inside the quilt for a fold-finished effect. Slipstitch the edges together invisibly using matching thread.

Alternative Edge Finishes The antique Love Apple quilt shown in the photograph has a fold-finished edge, in which the top and bottom layers of the quilt have been folded inside the quilt and sewn together. This is a time- and money-saving technique, but it is not always satisfactory because it does not frame the quilt. You may prefer to edge the quilt in one of the alternative ways listed here.

The most popular edge finish is to add a separate binding. This takes a bit more time to prepare than a fold-finished edge, but it gives you the freedom to choose any colour you prefer, and it does serve to frame and contain the quilt. If you'd like to add a separate binding, you'll need ⅜ m/yd of the fabric of your choice – red or green would work beautifully for this quilt. Cut this fabric into nine strips, each 3.8 cm/1½ in wide, and sew them together so that the strip measures 10¼ m/yds long. Instructions for applying a separate binding are on p. 131.

Self-binding is a quick and easy way to finish a quilt. However, this technique is not always recommended when the back is made from the same fabric as the border because a self-binding can make the edges of the quilt seem to fade away, especially if the colours of the rest of the quilt are strong. If you decide to self-bind your quilt, mark and cut an extra 2.54 cm/1 in all around the edge of the fabric for the back – this will add 5 cm/2 in to the length and width measurements. For this project you would need to cut one central panel 111.7 × 237.4 cm/44 × 93½ in; cut the side panels as directed on p. 106. Arrange the wadding/batting and the quilt top carefully over the quilt back to leave the 2.54 cm/1 in wide border free around the edges. After the quilting is done, finger-press the edges of the back 1.3 cm/½ in over to the wrong side of the fabric to make a folded edge. Then wrap the back onto the top, covering the edges of the wadding/batting and the quilt top and mitring the corners.

Piping will strengthen an edge and add a thin line of colour as well (see p. 115 for instructions).

Berry Block

Women living on the east coast of America began to have more leisure time to devote to their needlework in the latter half of the 19th century. Because patchwork quilts, other than masterpieces, were considered utilitarian, these women turned their attention and skills to making appliqué quilts. Intricate designs were appliquéd either onto a large piece of cloth or onto square blocks which were then sewn together to make up a quilt top. Graceful appliquéd borders were often added, and the quilt was finished off with splendid and elaborate quilting.

Making a masterpiece quilt was an excellent way for a woman to show off her needlework prowess, and the smallest details were scrutinized – each seam was perfect, every stitch was tiny and even. Late 19th-century appliqué quilts achieved such a degree of elegance that after years spent on making a single quilt, the quiltmaker was loathe to use it for anything other than a special occasion. Thus the tradition of the "best quilt" was born.

Much time and attention was lavished on making best quilts. Whenever possible, they were worked on only during the day when the light was excellent. Best quilts were not used every day, but were put on display occasionally for important events such as weddings, visits from the doctor or the minister, or to grace the beds of distinguished visitors. As a result, many magnificent quilts, such as this Berry Quilt, which was made in Kentucky around 1870, survive in excellent condition, because they were lovingly cared for and not extensively used.

A Berry quilt from Kentucky hangs from the gallery, while at ground level a Cherry Basket quilt is draped over a rush chair. The Stars quilt on the back of the sofa was made in Texas in 1855. The quilt maker used some fabrics that were imported from England, along with others that were manufactured in American mills.

Appliqué Designs

Ability level: Experienced

Size

Block: 43 cm/17 in square; 12 blocks
and 8 half-blocks required
Finished Quilt: 220.98 × 220.98 cm/87
× 87 in square

Materials

10¼ m/yds white fabric (includes
fabric for back of quilt and borders)

2¼ m/yds red fabric (includes fabric
for binding)

3½ m/yds green fabric (includes ¼
m/yd fabric for optional piping)

222.2 × 222.2 cm/87½ × 87½ in
piece of wadding/batting

Templates for: Background Block A:
44.4 × 44.4 cm/17½ × 17½ in
square; Background Half-Block B:
22.8 × 44.4 cm/9 × 17½ in.

Quilt Plan

Quilt Block

Cutting

Note: A 6 mm/¼ in seam allowance
is included in all measurements;
pattern pieces do not include a seam
allowance.

Quilt Back: 2 pieces, 111.7 × 222.2
cm/44 × 87½ in, white fabric.

Borders: 2 F strips 25.4 × 173.9 cm/10
× 68½ in, white fabric; 2 G strips
25.4 × 222.2 cm/10 × 87½ in, white
fabric.

C Stems: From green fabric, cut 9
2.54 cm/1 in wide strips across the full
width of the fabric; cut strips into 15.2

cm/6 in lengths to make a total of 64
C stems.

H Stems: From green fabric, cut one
2.54 cm/1 in wide strip across half the
width of the fabric; cut this strip into
four 12 cm/4¾ in lengths to make the
H stems.

Bias Strip for Vines: From green fabric,
cut one 95.2 cm/37½ in square.
Following the instructions for bias
binding on p. 130, cut 2.54 cm/1 in
wide bias strips and sew together to
measure 11 m/yds long.

Bias Strip for Stems: From green fabric cut one 25.4 cm/10 in square. Following the instructions for bias binding on p. 130, cut 1.9 cm/¾ in wide bias strips and sew together to measure 4 m/yds long.

Piping (optional): Cut eight 2.54 cm/1 in wide strips across the full width of the green fabric; stitch strips together so piping strip measures 9¾ m/yds.

Binding: Cut eight 4 cm/1½ in wide strips across the full width of the red fabric; stitch strips together so binding measures 9¾ m/yds long.

Pattern Pieces: (Number of pieces for one block are in parenthesis. Patterns are on p. 154.) A: (1) 12 white; B: (1) 8 white; C: (4) 64 green; D: (60) 960 red; E: (8) 128 green. Border: D: 232 red; E: 88 green; H: 4 green.

Piecing a Berry Block

Note: It will be easier to arrange the appliqués on the background if you press the block in half horizontally and vertically. The creases formed will divide the block into four equal quarters.

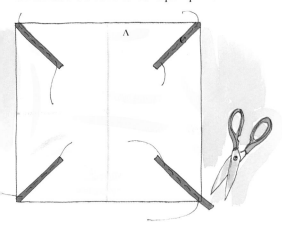

1 Fold the long raw edges of four C stems 6 mm/¼ in to the wrong side and press carefully. Place one stem at a 45 degree angle in each corner of an A background block. Baste in place, then trim off the ends of the stems extending beyond the corners of the background block.

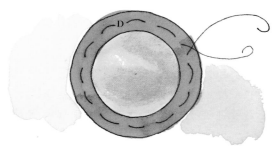

2 Prepare 60 D berries for appliqué as follows: Using matching thread, work a row of running stitches close to the edge of a fabric circle. Make a thin cardboard template for D *without* the 6 mm/¼ in seam allowance. Place the cardboard template in the exact middle of the fabric circle on the wrong side of the fabric.

3 Gently pull the basting stitches to gather the edge of the fabric circle around the cardboard template. Press the gathered circle gently so that there are no puckers or pleats on the right side. Then, carefully pop the template out of the fabric circle without distorting the pressed shape. The berry is ready to appliqué to the fabric. Note: It would be best to prepare all the berries at the same time. You will need to make several more cardboard templates as they will probably become distorted from the steam-pressing. You can store the prepared berries in a small cardboard box until you need them.

4 Arrange five berries in a straight row across the top of each C stem, covering the end of the stem with the central berry. Baste the berries in place. Use a ruler to check that each row is straight.

5 Arrange the remainder of the berries in four more rows, staggering the berries in between the others to make a neat triangular shape at the end of each stem. Baste in place, then appliqué the berries to the background using matching thread.

6 Prepare the E leaves for appliqué as directed on p. 129 (also see Appliquéd Leaves on p. 107 for the tips of the leaves); do not turn the ends under as they will be hidden beneath the stems. Position one leaf on each side of each stem; appliqué the leaves and then the stems in place using matching thread.

Appliqué Designs

7 Construct 11 more Berry Blocks in the same manner.

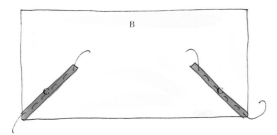

Half-Blocks

8 Prepare two C stems as described in Step 1. Position both stems along one long edge of a B half-block at a 45 degree angle; baste in place.

9 Prepare 30 D berries for appliqué as described in Steps 2 and 3. Arrange and appliqué to the background block as described in Steps 4 and 5.

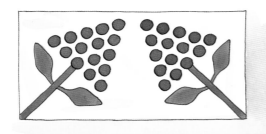

10 Prepare four E leaves for appliqué and position on each side of each stem as shown. Appliqué the

leaves and then the stems to the background block using matching thread.

11 Construct seven more half-blocks in the same manner.

12 Following the Quilt Plan on p. 112 and working on a large flat surface, arrange the whole blocks in three horizontal rows with four blocks in each row. Then arrange the half-blocks at the top and bottom of the whole blocks with the stems facing the middle of the quilt. Stitch the whole blocks and half-blocks together in horizontal rows, then stitch the rows together, matching seams carefully at the intersections. Press carefully.

13 Sew the F border strips to each side edge of the quilt top.

14 Sew the G border strips to the top and bottom of the quilt top.

Appliquéd Border

15 To construct the appliquéd border, first study the Quilt Plan on p. 112 and Border Plan below to familiarize yourself with how the border is designed. The curving bias strip "vine" is divided into four

quarters, and arranged from each corner of the quilt out to the midpoint of each border. (Note: Extra fabric has been allowed for each vine so you can make the curves as deep or as shallow as you wish; simply cut off the excess fabric at each end of each vine when you're done.) Berries, stems and leaves are added after the vine has been basted in place.

16 First, mark the positions where the vines will end (near the middle of each border strip). Measure and mark the exact midpoint of each F and G border. Then measure 7.6 cm/3 in to the left and right of the midpoint and 10 cm/4 in away from the long raw edge of the quilt. Mark this position for the end point of each vine.

17 Cut four 248.9 cm/98 in pieces of the green bias "vine". Press both long edges of each vine 6 mm/¼ in to the wrong side, being careful not to stretch the strips out of shape as you press; do not press the ends under as they will be hidden. The vine will be 13 mm/½ in wide. You may find it easier to make a 6 mm/¼ in wide cardboard strip to use as a guide for pressing.

18 Fold the vine in half to find the middle and mark with a pin, then pin the middle of the vine to one

High-relief Appliqué

To emphasize the berries on the border or the blocks, stuff them to create a raised, sculptural effect. To do this, cut out twice the number of berries required, adding a 6 mm/¼ in seam allowance. Stitch two berries

together with right sides facing and raw edges even. Using sharp scissors, clip into one fabric only (the facing) to make an opening for turning. Turn berry to the right side through the opening, smoothing the edges with your fingers. Press so that the seam

does not show on the right side. Stuff the berry until plump, pushing the stuffing evenly into all areas. Lap the cut edges over one another and whip-stitch together, then position the appliqué on the background, facing side down. Slipstitch in place.

Border Plan

corner of the quilt top, about 9.5 cm/3¾ in away from the corner. Following the Quilt Plan on p. 112 and Border Plan, bottom left, and working slowly and carefully, arrange the vine along the F and G borders making three curves as shown and ending at the points you marked in Step 16. When you are satisfied with the curves, baste the vine to the border, then press very carefully so that the curves are smooth and unpuckered. Repeat for the other three corners of the quilt.

19 Prepare the remaining 88 leaves and 232 berries for appliqué as you did for the blocks. Store the appliqués in a cardboard box until you need them.

20 For the corner berry units, press both long edges and one short edge of the H stems 6 mm/¼ in to the wrong side. The short edge must be pressed under because it will not be covered with a berry; see the Border Plan on the opposite page.

21 Tuck the unfinished end of one H stem beneath the vine, in the exact middle of one corner curve, positioning the stem at a 45 degree angle as shown; baste in place. Arrange four berries across the top of the stem in a straight row. Then arrange six more berries in three additional rows, staggering the berries in between the others as shown in the Border Plan. Baste the berries in place. Position two leaves on each side of the stem, tucking the ends beneath the stem. Appliqué the corner berry unit to the border using matching thread. Repeat for the other three corners.

22 Next, arrange six berries and two leaves at each end of each curved vine (at the midpoint of each border strip) as shown in the Quilt Plan and the Border Plan opposite. First arrange three berries in a straight row across the end of the vine, using a ruler to ensure that the berries are straight. Then stagger the other berries in two more rows as shown; baste. Position the leaves along each side of the vine as shown. Baste in place, then appliqué the pieces to the border using matching thread.

23 Cut 24 15.8 cm/6¼ in pieces of the green bias strip for the stems of the remaining berry units; press both long edges 6 mm/¼ in to the wrong side. Position the stems along the vine as shown in the Quilt Plan and the Border Plan opposite, curving the stems slightly. Arrange six berries at the end of each stem and two leaves on each side of each stem as shown. Appliqué the pieces to the border using matching thread.

24 Finally, appliqué the remaining 16 leaves to the side of the vine opposite the berry units as shown in the Quilt Plan and Border Plan.

Assembling and Finishing the Quilt
25 To construct the quilt back, sew the two fabric pieces together along the long edges. Press the seam allowance to one side.

26 Assemble the quilt top, wadding/batting and back as directed on p. 130.

27 Outline-quilt the berries, leaves, stems and vines. For extra definition, quilt a crosshatch design in the white areas between the groups of berries. See Step 8 on p. 125 for instructions on how to mark the crosshatching lines on the quilt.

28 The quilt shown in the photograph is piped with green fabric and then bound in red. If you do not wish to add piping, go on to Step 32. If you wish to add piping, centre the piping cord on the wrong side of the piping fabric, then fold the fabric in half lengthwise, enclosing the cord. Using a zipper foot on the sewing machine, stitch the folded fabric together close to the cord. Trim the seam allowance to 6 mm/¼ in.

29 Pin the piping to the right side of the quilt top with all raw edges even, beginning in the middle of one edge of the quilt. When you reach the first

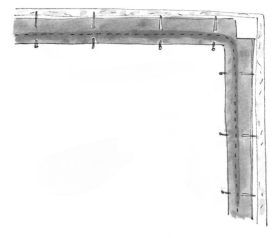

corner, ease the piping around the corner by clipping into the seam allowance of the piping exactly at the point where it will turn the corner as shown. Continue pinning the piping to the quilt top until you reach the beginning.

30 Overlap the beginning of the piping by 2.54 cm/ 1 in, then cut away any excess piping. Remove 2.54 cm/1 in of the stitching from the end of the piping, push back the excess fabric and trim away only the cord so that the beginning and end of the cord are flush. Now straighten out the excess empty fabric and finger-press the raw edge 13 mm/½ in to the inside.

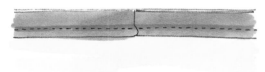

31 Slip the beginning of the piping inside the end so the raw ends are covered; smooth the fold of the fabric with your fingers so it looks like a seam. Pin in place. Stitch the piping to the quilt as close to the cord as possible using a zipper foot.

32 Bind the quilt with a separate binding as directed on p. 131. If you have piped the quilt, secure the binding to the quilt using a zipper foot and stitching as close to the cord as possible.

Quilting Designs

It is a well-known fact that a quilt, no matter how elaborately pieced or appliquéd, only comes to life when the quilting stitches are added. As with most other needlework techniques, our forebears managed to turn their quilting stitches into a fine art. On some of the antique quilts in this book, the tiny, even quilting stitches are as small as 18 to the inch! Before you feel defeated, remember that the padding in old quilts is much thinner than is commonly used today, and also, those women had been sewing from an early age. As long as your stitches are even and attractive on the front and the back of the quilt, feel proud of your efforts.

To simulate the appearance of an aged quilt, use a cotton wadding/batting, which will give a flatter result. When using a cotton filler, you must not leave an area larger than 5 cm/ 2 in unquilted. For a more three-dimensional effect, use polyester wadding/batting, which can be bought in virtually any size and which does not have to be as closely quilted – every 7.6 cm/3 in will suffice. Silk and wool fillers are also available, but must be handled with care, and close quilting is essential to prevent the filling from shifting. Some of the quilts in this book were padded with old quilts or blankets. Others were filled with hand-carded cotton – this is evident when you hold a quilt up to the light and see the tiny black specks which are the cotton seeds.

The wedding quilts on the rustic painted chairs from Provence were made around 1850. Known as courtepointes, *these were usually made by the bride's mother using a scarf that is printed on only three sides; on the fourth side, a matching strip of printed fabric was added. An additional plain border was added to the quilt on the right.*

Corded Trapunto

The golden quilt draped over the back of the bench seems to glow with the sunshine of Marseille in France, where it was made in about 1880. The simple square-diamond quilting in the middle of the quilt contrasts with the striking border which has worked in corded quilting and Trapunto or stuffed quilting. The meandering vine and the parallel channels bordering the leaves have been corded, while the leaves and berries have been stuffed in order to give them a sculptural effect. You can create a beautiful border just by quilting this design in the normal way (see p. 130). However, if you wish to achieve the three-dimensional quality of this glorious quilt, you can add corded quilting and Trapunto in addition to the layer of wadding/batting.

For the cording, you should use thick cotton piping cord that has been preshrunk. And for the Trapunto, you should choose a loosely woven fabric for the back so that the threads can be separated without tearing them. The filling is inserted through the opening, then the threads are pushed back into their original position.

The simple patchwork area in the middle of the quilt is composed of fabric scraps. To achieve a similar effect, use up your scraps to make each square in a combination of a light and a dark fabric. Or, if you are working from new material, use the same fabric for the light and dark pieces throughout the quilt as illustrated in the Quilt Plan overleaf; the exact yardage for this is given overleaf.

The fabrics in the quilts shown here are from Provence, which is also where the quilts were made. These stunning examples are on display at the Tarascon museum run by the Souleaido fabric company.

Quilting Designs

Ability level: Intermediate

Size

Square: 8.8 cm/3½in; 196 squares required

Finished Quilt: 205.7 cm/81 in square

Materials

4½ m/yds medium fabric for borders

4½ m/yds loosely woven floral fabric for quilt back

1¼ m/yds light fabric or fabric scraps

1¼ m/yds dark fabric or fabric scraps

207 cm/81½ in square of wadding/ batting (includes seam allowance)

73 m/yds thick piping cord (optional)

polyester fibrefill or cotton (optional)

thick blunt yarn needle (optional)

Quilt Plan

Border Plan

Cutting

Note: A 6 mm/¼ in seam allowance is included in all measurements; pattern pieces do not include a seam allowance.

Quilt Back: 2 pieces, 104.1 × 207 cm/ 41 × 81½in, floral fabric.

Borders: 4 strips 41.9 × 207cm/16½ × 81½in, medium fabric.

Pattern pieces: (Number of pieces for a single square are in parenthesis. Pattern is on p. 155.) A: (1) 196 light; A: (1) 196 dark.

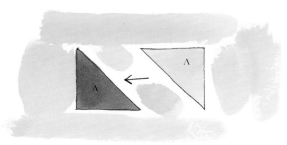

Piecing a Patchwork Square

1 Sew each light A to a dark A along the diagonal edge to form a square. Press the seam allowance toward the dark fabric.

2 Construct 195 more patchwork squares in the same manner.

Assembling and Marking the Quilt

3 Following the Quilt Plan and working on a large flat surface, arrange the patchwork squares in 14 rows with 14 squares in each row. Turn the squares as shown in the Quilt Plan, or arrange them to your own satisfaction.

4 Sew the squares together in rows, then sew the rows together, matching seams carefully at the intersections.

5 Stitch a border to each side of the quilt top, allowing the ends to extend beyond the top for mitring. Then stitch a border to the top and bottom edges in the same manner.

6 Mitre the corners of the borders following the directions on p. 130.

7 Mark the quilting design on the right side of the quilt top as directed on p.142-3 and Steps 8-12 below.

8 Measure and mark a straight line on the border 8.8 cm/3½ in away from the patchwork all around the quilt top. Mark three more lines parallel to the first, each spaced 6 mm/¼ in apart.

9 Study the Quilt Plan, the Border Plan and the photograph on the previous page to see how the quilting lines work in the middle of the quilt. Mark

the diagonal quilting lines across the entire central portion of the quilt top, within the parallel lines marked on the border. Mark the diagonal lines in groups of three, spacing each of these lines 13 mm/ ½ in apart. The square formed by the intersection of the lines is 6.9 × 6.9 cm/2¾ × 2¾ in.

The easiest way to begin is to mark the first diagonal lines at each edge of one corner square, with the additional parallel lines marked *within* that square. Then, mark the rest of the lines on the quilt top working away from the outer lines of these two central sets of lines.

10 Mark diagonal lines perpendicular to the lines marked in Step 9 in the same manner.

11 Enlarge the leaf and berry quilting pattern on p. 142 following the instructions for enlarging designs given on p. 141. Transfer the pattern to the border all around the quilt top, with the inner leaves just touching the outer parallel line that was previously marked. First mark each corner, then connect the corners by drawing a gently curving vine, following the Quilt Plan and Border Plan. Add the leaves and berries as shown.

12 Mark five parallel lines, each spaced 6 mm/¼ in apart around the edge of the quilt top. The inner line should just touch the edges of the leaves of the border quilting pattern.

13 To construct the quilt back, sew the two fabric pieces together along the long edges. Press the seam allowance to one side.

14 Assemble the quilt top, wadding/batting and back as directed on p. 130.

Quilting and Finishing

15 Quilt along the marked lines of the design, working from the middle of the quilt out to the edges. Before you quilt the last two parallel lines at the outer edges of the quilt, fold the raw edges of the quilt top and the quilt back 6 mm/¼ in inside the

quilt, enclosing all raw edges and the wadding/ batting. Slipstitch the edges together invisibly. Then finish the last two rows of quilting.

16 If you wish to add cording to the vine and to the straight channels on the border, thread a blunt yarn needle with thick piping cord. Work from the back of the quilt. To begin, insert the needle point between the back of the fabric and the wadding/ batting. Be careful not to penetrate through to the right side of the quilt. Push the needle through the channel, making each stitch as long as is comfortable according to the length of the needle that you are using. Pull the needle and the cord gently through the channel, leaving a 13 mm/½ in tail at the beginning. To work curves, bring the needle out at the point where you would be bending the fabric. Reinsert the needle into the same hole and continue guiding it through the channel. Pull the cord through gently but do not pull it taut; leave a small loop at each exit point.

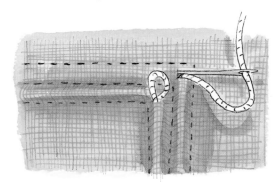

17 To turn a corner, bring the needle out at the corner point and reinsert it again in the same hole. Following Step 16, guide the needle through the channel in the new direction. Do not pull the cord taut, but leave a small loop at the exit point. When the work is finished, grasp opposite corners of the quilt firmly and pull diagonally, first in one direction, and then the other; this will allow the cord to settle into the channels and to remove any puckers that may have formed.

18 To stuff the berries and leaves, read and follow the instructions for Trapunto on p. 131. Continue until all the berries and leaves have been stuffed.

North Country Quilt

Throughout the second half of the 19th century and into the 20th, quilts were in conventional use in most homes in the north of England. The climate and economic times meant that making a bed quilt was a necessary part of life. The quilts that took pride of place were "wholecloth" quilts, or those made from plain lengths of material which showed off the quilting stitches to perfection. Patchwork was out of favour and never used for the front of a quilt, just the back, and only then out of absolute necessity. White material was considered the most desirable, as there was nothing to detract from the flawlessness of the stitches. Although many of these wholecloth, heavily quilted works are known collectively as "Durham quilts", they were actually made throughout the north of England, as well as in Scotland and Wales.

It was at this time that professional quilters and pattern-makers came into their own. Professional quilt stampers would mark the full design of a wholecloth quilt on the fabric for a fee. Talented stampers such as George Gardiner and Elizabeth Sanderson became household names; their quilts have an easily recognized distinctive style.

This cream sateen quilt has a bordered design reminiscent of the style of George Gardiner. The central medallion is filled with flowers and feathers, while the background has a square diamond infill pattern. The design is contained by swagged borders and corners that match the medallion. The quilt at the foot of the bed is called Devil's Claws.

Quilting Designs

Ability level: Experienced

Size

Finished quilt 208.3 × 256.5 cm/82 ×
101 in

Materials

11¾ m/yds solid colour fabric (includes fabric for back and binding)

Greaseproof paper or tracing paper

Blunt yarn needle and a cork

209.5 × 257.8 cm/82½ × 101½ in
piece of wadding/batting (includes
seam allowance)

Quilt Plan

Corner Design

Central Motif

Cutting

Note: A 6 mm/¼ in seam allowance
is included in all measurements.

Quilt Front: From solid colour fabric
one central panel, 111.7 × 257.8 cm/
44 × 101½ in; 2 side panels, 50.1 ×
257.8 cm/19¾ × 101½ in.

Quilt back: 2 pieces, 105.4 × 257.8cm/
41½ × 101½ in solid-colour fabric.

Binding

Cut nine 4 cm/1½ in wide strips
across the full width of the remaining
fabric; stitch strips together so binding measures 10⅜ m/yds long.

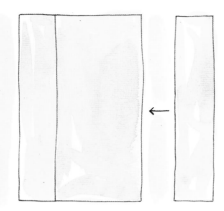

Piecing a Wholecloth Quilt

1 To construct the quilt front, sew a narrow panel to each side of the full-width panel of fabric, matching the long edges. If the fabrics have a sheen, make sure that grain is running in the same direction when you sew the pieces together. Press the seam allowances to one side.

2 To construct the quilt back, sew the two fabric pieces together along the long edges, making sure that the grain is running the same way if the fabric has a sheen. Press the seam allowance to one side.

Marking the Quilt

3 Enlarge the quilting patterns on pp. 144 and 145 as directed on p. 141. Refer to the Quilt Plan as you are drawing the designs.

4 Working on a large flat surface, cut and tape pieces of greaseproof paper or tracing paper together so the paper measures 208.3 × 256.5 cm/ 82 × 101 in. Draw a line across the full length and width of the paper, dividing the paper in half horizontally and vertically.

5 Place the enlarged quarter-pattern for the central motif beneath the greaseproof paper or tracing paper, lining up the dash lines of the design with the horizontal and vertical lines of the paper. Trace the quarter design carefully onto the large sheet of paper. Then reverse the design by flipping it over and transfer to the next quarter. Continue in this way until you have transferred the entire central motif to the paper.

6 Next position the enlarged corner design in one of the corners of the paper and trace. The end of the corner stem should be 6 mm/¼ in away from the edge of the paper, with the swags and leaves parallel to the sides. Repeat for each of the other three corners.

7 Then trace the swags, leaves and flowers around the edges, drawing 6 swags across the top and bottom edges, and 8 swags along the sides.

8 Finally, fill in the area between the designs with a crosshatch pattern. First, mark straight parallel lines, spaced 2.54 cm/1 in apart from one corner to the opposite corner across the entire quilt (in between the marked designs). Then turn the quilt and mark the lines from corner to corner in the opposite direction.

9 To transfer the design lines to the right side of the quilt front, first place several layers of bedsheets on a large flat surface; the sheets should be slightly larger than the quilt. Make sure that the sheets are lying flat and smooth.

10 Find the middle of the quilt front by folding the fabric in half horizontally and then vertically; press lightly in the middle, then unfold. Then, place the quilt front, right side up, on the sheets. Smooth it carefully in place so that the corners are true, then pin to the sheets all around every 5 cm/2 in.

11 Place the traced design on top of the quilt front with the pencil side uppermost, placing the exact middle of the design over the pressed middle of the quilt front. Pin to the quilt front and sheets, making sure that there are no creases in the fabrics. Pin all around the edges. Then, pin across the design horizontally and vertically, then diagonally.

12 Using the side of a blunt yarn needle (with the eye end inserted into a cork to make it easier to grip), carefully go over the pattern lines to needle-mark the design onto the fabric. Press firmly using the side of the point to prevent ripping the fabric. This will cut the tracing paper so you will not be able to use the pattern again.

13 If you are quilting the design on a frame and it will basically be left undisturbed, the needlemarked design lines should be enough for you to follow. However, if you are quilting with a hoop or if the quilt will be folded and transported somewhere else, you should go over the needlemarked lines with a coloured pencil that is slightly darker than the fabric. These lines are a bit easier to follow than just the needlemarking, and should disappear once the quilting is done.

Assembling and Finishing the Quilt

14 Assemble the quilt top, wadding/batting and back as directed on p. 130.

15 Beginning near the middle of the quilt, quilt the crosshatching first until you establish a rhythm and a quilting stitch length that you are comfortable with. Then quilt all the marked design lines, working from the middle of the quilt out to the edges.

16 Bind the quilt with a separate binding as directed on p. 131.

Basic Techniques

This section covers the quiltmaking techniques required for making the dozen country-style quilts featured on pages 70-125. These quilts are not suitable for beginning quilters, either because the quilts have hundreds of pieces that need meticulous cutting and piecing, or because the intricate appliqué or quilting patterns would simply be too demanding for a beginner to try. However, it would be possible for a quilter with some experience to try the intermediate designs, then work up to the more experienced designs.

The basic instructions that follow assume that the reader has a familiarity with quilting terms and basic sewing skills. If you are a beginner and this book has inspired you to take up quiltmaking, you should refer to the Bibliography on page 162 for a list of books that will teach you the craft. Then, after you have mastered the basics you can try to make one or more of the magnificent quilts illustrated in this book, creating your own future heirloom.

Study the photographs and the Quilt Plans on pages 72-124 to choose the quilt that you wish to make. Then read through the instructions and review the step-by-step illustrations to make sure that you are capable of constructing the design. There is no point in starting a quilt that you find too difficult, as this will blind you to the pleasures of quilting and you are likely to end up with a project that you are not going to finish.

The rough wooden walls of a rustic cabin contrast well with the crisp white and navy blue fabrics in the 1890s patchwork quilt. The colours are an appropriate choice since the pattern is called Ocean Waves; it was made in West Virginia.

How to Begin

If you like a design and aren't sure whether you can tackle it, try making only one block or section of the quilt which will then become a cushion or pillow cover or a very small quilt. Use scraps so that you don't invest a lot of money in fabric, and have fun trying the design. If you are pleased with the results, then set about making the complete quilt.

The next step is to decide how big you want the quilt to be. Check the quilt sizes given with the instructions. If you wish to alter the size of a quilt, adjust the pattern by making more or less blocks or by adding or taking away borders. (Note: The North Country quilt can be reduced or enlarged in size by adjusting the position of the designs when you are drawing the pattern – you will then have more or less quilting in the background.) If you change the size of the quilt, you must adjust the fabric yardage as well.

Fabrics

Part of the charm of an antique quilt is its "old" appearance – the faded colours and the soft feel of the fabrics. If you are making a quilt from modern fabrics and wish to make it appear old, look for fabrics with a cream, beige or ecru background, or those in soft colours. You can also try using vegetable-based dyes to produce an aged effect on your existing fabrics.

Tea-dyeing has been a very popular way of treating fabrics to create an antique effect, but it is really not recommended for a quilt that you are making to last for many years. Tea contains tannic acid which will weaken the fibres in the fabric, making it vulnerable to early deterioration.

Because these are quilts for more experienced quilters, I've tried to refrain from specifying the colour of the fabrics that should be used to make the quilts, so as not to sway your choices. In many cases, the fabrics are simply called "light, medium, bright or dark". The colour scheme is entirely at your own discretion: feel free to copy the quilts in the colour photographs exactly, or make up your own colour scheme. The best way to choose your colours is to find one fabric that you absolutely love,

and then choose the other fabrics to work with it. For the best results, use 100 percent cotton fabrics of a similar weight.

It is recommended that you prewash your fabrics before cutting them out. Clip into the selvages to prevent uneven shrinkage, then put like-colours in the washing machine with a small amount of fabric softener if you wish; you needn't use detergent since the fabrics aren't dirty. Wash the fabrics in hot water, then hang to dry; drying in a machine may twist long lengths of fabric off grain. Press with a steam-iron. If, after washing, you are unsure about whether a fabric is colourfast, soak it in a solution of three parts cold water to one part white vinegar, then rinse until the water runs clear. Wash the fabric again with a piece of white fabric; if there is any sign of bleeding, discard the fabric.

Cutting the Fabrics

The fabric yardages that are given with each set of instructions assume very careful measuring and cutting. If you wish to add a margin of safety by buying some extra fabric, you can always use the leftover fabric in some future project. As a general rule, when cutting out the pieces, first cut the fabrics for the quilt back, then the borders, background blocks and binding. Cut the smaller patchwork or appliqué pieces from what remains.

All of the measurements given for cutting the larger pieces such as the quilt back, borders and binding, include a 6mm/¼in seam allowance. None of the templates include a seam allowance (to save space in the book), so be sure to add a 6mm/¼in seam allowance either to the template or to the fabric when you are marking the pieces.

Instructions on making and using the templates are given on pages 149-150. When you are marking the pieces that need to be cut on your fabrics, use a well-sharpened pencil and a ruler. Take your time and be very accurate with your marking and cutting; this will save time and trouble later when you are trying to fit everything together!

Rotary cutting is a fast and easy way to cut straight pieces such as squares, rectangles and triangles, as well as borders and bindings. You will

need a rotary cutter with a large wheel, a rotary ruler (which is made from thick clear plastic) and a self-healing mat (available from art supply and quilt shops). To prepare the fabric, fold it in half on the straight grain with the selvages matching; steam-press the layers together. Fold in half again, matching the first fold to the selvages and creating four layers; steam-press again. Carefully pick up the pressed fabric without unfolding it and place it on the cutting mat. Position the rotary ruler on the fabric, aligning one of the grid lines on the ruler with the pressed and folded edge of the fabric (the one opposite the selvage edge). Pressing down firmly on the ruler with one hand, run the blade of the rotary cutter along the edge of the ruler; this will trim off any ragged edges and straighten the fabric on grain; see below. For safety, always push the blade away from you when cutting fabrics.

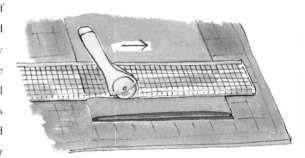

To cut strips of fabric, first decide upon the width of the strips you require, then add 13mm/½in for seam allowances. Note: The measurements given with the instructions already include seam allowances. Position the ruler on the fabric so that your cutting edge is the required distance from the straightened edge of the fabric.

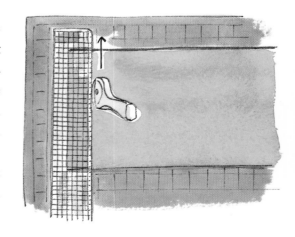

Pressing firmly down on the ruler and cutter, run the blade along the edge of the ruler to cut the strip. To cut squares, trim one edge of the strip to remove the folds. Turn the strip and measure the same distance as the width of the strip from the cut end; cut along this measurement for four perfect squares.

How to Sew Patchwork

All of the quilts can be pieced by hand or machine. When sewing the pieces together, match the raw edges carefully, pinning them together at each end if necessary to prevent shifting. Always stitch pieces together making a 6mm/¼in seam allowance. Sew the pieces together in a chain without breaking the thread to save both time and thread. Press the seam allowances to one side, preferably toward the darker fabric; pressing is especially crucial when trying to match seams or points. When sewing sub-units together, carefully match the seams before you sew, pinning the pieces at crucial points. When matching seams, particularly when joining the rows of blocks together, press the seam allowances in opposite directions to reduce bulk.

How to Inset

Insetting is when a patchwork piece is sewn into the angled area formed by the joining of two other pieces. A number of the patchwork designs in this book require insetting, and although the procedure is tricky and time-consuming, being able to inset will enable you to make some really spectacular designs, so it is well worth learning how to do it!

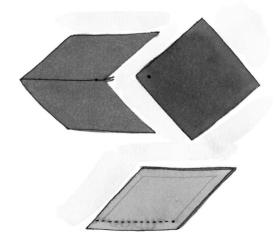

Following the illustration, above, join the pieces forming the angle by sewing them together; end

your stitching exactly 6mm/¼in from the edge to be inset (shown by a dot).

Pin the piece to be inset to one edge of the angle and stitch slowly and carefully from the inside (starting exactly at the seam) to the outside edge in the direction of the arrow.

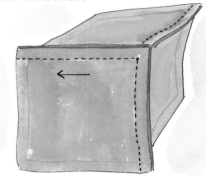

Then pin the piece to be inset to the adjacent angle. Stitch from the inside to the outside edge following the arrow, and beginning your stitching exactly where the other line of stitching began (at the seam). Open out the fabrics and carefully steam-press. If you notice any puckers at the corner, you can usually eliminate them by removing a stitch from one of the seams just sewn.

How to Sew Curves

The secret to sewing curved patches successfully is to cut the pieces with the curves on the bias; then the pieces are easy to manipulate and fit together.

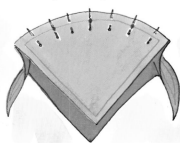

Mark the seam allowances and the notches (for matching) on the wrong side of the fabric pieces. Pin the pieces together, matching the notches and the side edges first. Then ease the remainder of the bias edges to fit, using as many pins as necessary. Stitch the pieces together smoothly, then open out and steam-press carefully.

How to Appliqué

Some of the most beautiful and prized country quilts are appliquéd, in which the designs are made by placing (or applying) one piece of fabric on top of another. These quilts are almost entirely sewn by hand, which makes them very time-consuming, but always greatly admired.

To prepare the pieces for appliqué, first mark and cut out the templates as directed on pages 149-150. After the pieces have been cut out, use the tip of a sharp pair of scissors to clip into the curved edges of the appliqué perpendicular to the marked outline of the piece as shown below; do not clip beyond the marked line.

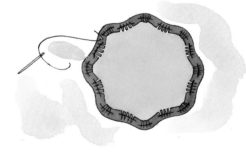

Make extra clips along deep curves for ease in turning. Straight edges need not be clipped. Then, turn the raw edges of the appliqués 6mm/¼in to the wrong side and hand-baste in place. Steam-press the folded edges carefully.

Pin, then baste the appliqués in position on the background fabric. When you are satisfied with the arrangement, slipstitch the appliqués to the background, using matching thread and making tiny invisible stitches; see below.

Basic Techniques

How to Make Bias Strips and Bindings

To make bias strips either for appliquéd vines or for for binding a quilt, cut a square of fabric to the required size on the straight grain of the fabric. (Note: When a long length of bias is required, you may be instructed to cut more than one square of fabric. Treat each square separately, following the instructions to make the bias, then join the ends of the bias strips to make the required length.)

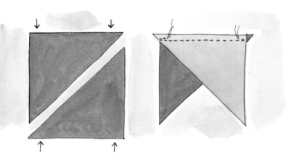

Following the diagram above, cut the fabric in half diagonally, then with the right sides facing, stitch the edges indicated by arrows together, making a 6mm/¼in seam. Press the seam allowance open, then trim the seam allowance to 3mm/⅛in. Following the individual instructions for the required width, mark parallel lines across the seamed fabric as shown in the diagram below.

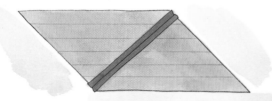

Take care not to stretch the fabric as you mark it, and use a very sharp pencil and an accurate ruler.

Following the diagram above, pin the diagonal edges of the marked fabric together with right-sides

facing, offsetting the edges so that the top edge of the fabric aligns with the first marked line. Match the marked lines as you pin the edges together. Then stitch together, making a 6mm/¼in seam. Press the seam allowance open, then trim to 3mm/⅛in. Beginning at the top edge, cut the fabric along the marked lines in one continuous spiral as shown in the diagram below. Take care in handling the bias strip as it will stretch easily.

How to Mitre Corners

Stitch the border strips to the quilt top with right sides facing, making a 6mm/¼in seam; allow the excess border fabric to extend evenly beyond each edge of the quilt top. Press the border strips to the right side.

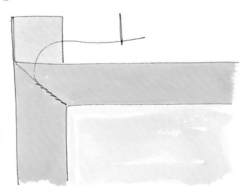

Following the diagram above, fold one border strip back on itself, forming a 45 degree angle; press and pin in place. Then stitch the folded edge of the border to its counterpart either by hand from the right side, or by machine from the wrong side. Press carefully, then trim both seam allowances to 13mm/½in.

Assembling a Quilt

A quilt is composed of a sandwich of three layers: the quilt top, the wadding/batting and the back. To assemble the layers, you will need a large, clean flat

surface, preferably a wooden or tiled floor, although a carpeted floor will suffice.

First, steam-press the quilt top and quilt back very carefully. This will be the last time these fabrics can be pressed, so do a good job. Remove any frayed edges or threads from the wrong side of the fabrics. If there are any bulky areas, clip away excess fabric carefully from the wrong side.

Place the quilt back, wrong side up, on a large flat surface, smoothing it carefully in place. If you can, use masking tape to secure the edges to the surface and keep the back taut. Next, place the wadding/batting carefully on top of the quilt back, centring it between all the side edges. Finally, place the quilt top, right side up, over the wadding/batting, again smoothing it carefully in place. Baste layers together horizontally, vertically and diagonally, working from the middle out to the edges. If the quilt will be moved around a lot or if you are planning to use a hoop, add extra rows of concentric basting to hold the three layers together securely; see below.

Do not skimp on basting the quilt; there is nothing worse than having to unpick your quilting stitches because the quilt back has developed an unsightly fold! If you are in any doubt, add an extra row of basting.

How to Quilt

It is best to use a frame or hoop for quilting to maintain an even tension; this will help make your stitches even and consistent. Insert your basted quilt sandwich in a hoop or a frame. Cut a 46cm/18in length of quilting thread and insert in a size 8 (or smaller) "Between" needle; knot the end. Insert the needle through the quilt top and wadding/

batting and pull the thread through, giving the thread a sharp tug so that the knot pops below the quilt top and becomes embedded in the wadding/batting. Using a thimble on the middle finger of your sewing hand, begin working a series of small running stitches as shown in the diagram below.

Either follow the quilting pattern marked on the quilt top or outline-quilt the pieces as directed in the individual instructions. Point the needle at an angle through the quilt so that it touches your index finger positioned below the quilt; use that finger to guide the needle back up to the quilt top. Make sure that you keep an even tension on the thread, and that each stitch goes through all three layers of fabric. To end a line of stitching, make a small knot in the thread near the surface of the quilt top, then make a small stitch and tug the knot beneath the surface; clip the thread end close to the surface so that it disappears inside the quilt sandwich.

Trapunto Quilting

To do Trapunto quilting, first construct a stuffing implement by inserting the eye-end of a blunt yarn needle into a cork. Begin by making an opening for the stuffing. Holding the stuffing implement at an angle, gently insert the point in between the woven threads in the middle of the area to be stuffed.

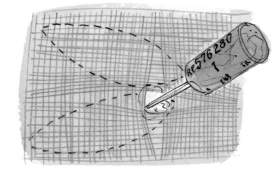

Wriggle the point to enlarge the opening without breaking the threads.

Following the diagram below left, insert small wisps of stuffing through the opening a little at a time, until the area is stuffed. Use the point of the needle to gently push the bits of stuffing out to the edges. After the area has been stuffed, use the point of the needle to gently coax the threads around the opening back into their original position.

Binding a Quilt

Separate Binding Press one long edge of the binding strip 6mm/¼in to the wrong side. Begin in the middle of one side of the quilt. Fold the end of the binding 13mm/½in to the wrong side, then place on the quilt top with right sides facing and raw

edges even. Begin machine stitching the binding to the quilt, making a 6mm/¼in seam.

Following the diagram above, stitch to the first corner, making smaller stitches as you approach the corner. When the needle is exactly 6mm/¼in from the edge of the quilt, stop stitching, leaving needle in the corner point. Raise the presser foot of the sewing machine and pivot the quilt on the needle to prepare to sew the next edge. Adjust the binding so that the raw edge is parallel to the next edge of the quilt. A tuck will form in the binding; do not catch this tuck in the stitching, but allow it to lie out of the way – this excess fabric will be used to mitre the corner. Lower the presser foot and continue stitching with small stitches for about 13mm/½in. Adjust the stitch length to normal and continue stitching to the next corner.

Stitch the remainder of the binding to the quilt, sewing each corner in the same way. Trim the binding at the end, leaving 13mm/½in which will

overlap the beginning of the binding. Wrap the binding over to the quilt back, covering the stitching line. Slipstitch the binding to the quilt back using matching thread. Fold the excess fabric at the corners neatly at a 45 degree angle and stitch in place for a mitred corner.

Self-Binding When a quilt has a self-binding, the back is larger than the quilt top and the wadding/batting. The excess fabric around the edges of the back is folded over onto the quilt top and stitched in place (see above).

Trim the quilt top and the wadding/batting evenly. Measure to make sure that the quilt back extends 1.9cm/¾in beyond the quilt top all around. Following the diagram above, fold the raw edges of the quilt back 6mm/¼in to the wrong side. Wrap the back over onto the quilt top, covering the raw edges of the wadding/batting and the top; pin in place, mitring the corners. Slipstitch the folded edge of the back invisibly to the quilt top using matching thread.

Signing the Quilt

Always sign and date your quilts. Embroider your name and the date on a small piece of fabric either in cross-stitch or outline stitch. Or, you can write or type your name on the fabric with indelible ink. Hem all the edges of the fabric label, then stitch to the back of the quilt using matching thread.

Alternatively, you can quilt or embroider your name and the date on the front of the quilt, making your signature and the date into part of the overall design.

Care of Quilts

A quilt that is used for any decorative purpose is exposed to many different factors that will contribute to its deterioration. The best way to care for your quilts is to prevent anything from happening to them in the first place. Take proper precautions and your quilts will last a long time without any need for drastic measures to keep them in fine condition. Cleaning a quilt should be your last option.

A quilt will receive the least amount of stress when it is kept flat, so one of the best ways to store or display a quilt is by placing it on a bed. However, the position of the bed is extremely important. Is it in direct sunlight? Is it touching a wall that may be damp or situated in a room that leaks when it rains? Is the bed near a window that draws in excessive dust and dirt, such as exhaust fumes·from a busy street? Will the bed be used by the family pet? Do rodents or insects have easy access to the room? Exposing a quilt to any of these situations will speed up the disintegration of the textile fibres, and your prized possession will soon be in tatters.

Light is the worst culprit. One of the enjoyable aspects of living in a country-style home is being able to fling open the windows to let in the fresh air and sunshine. But if an antique quilt is exposed to even a few hours of sunlight or subjected to continual light from a fluorescent lamp, the dyes will fade and the fibres become brittle and dry which can cause them to split and fall apart. Damage from light is irreversible and the more a quilt is exposed to light, the worse the damage will be.

Typical examples of late 19th-century American patchwork and appliqué quilts are carefully stored in a pie safe. A layer of acid-free paper protects the quilts from the acidic wood of the shelves.

There are several ways to prevent light from harming a quilt. The most obvious is to never, ever place a quilt in direct light – whether from the sun or an indoor light source. Even if your antique quilt rack fits best in front of your bay window, don't be tempted to ruin your quilt by placing it there. One solution is to place thick draperies over the windows to shield a quilt from sunlight. This may not be satisfactory if you wish to live in a bright and sunny space. Another way is to use Mylar polyester film or some other ultraviolet light filtering system on your windows and glass doors. Some of these shields, when placed directly on the glass, are virtually invisible yet will serve to protect a quilt from sunlight. You can also buy shields and sleeves for indoor lighting (see the Directory for a list of suppliers). However, no shields will protect indefinitely against a continual light source, which is why the position of your quilt in a room is so important – keep it as far away from light sources as you possibly can.

Water causes permanent damage. If a quilt is kept in a wet or continually damp situation – either by being stored in a leaky attic, basement or garage, or against a damp wall inside the house – mould and mildew will form, causing an unpleasant odour and irrevocable damage. Keep all quilts in a comfortable temperature in a dry place. Never store a quilt in a plastic bag.

Dust is an almost invisible enemy, yet a build-up of dust particles can actually cut through fragile fibres and threads. However, this is probably the easiest problem to fix because most quilts can withstand careful vacuuming. It is recommended that you vacuum your quilts regularly – at least every six months if they are on display (see page 137 for instructions).

Quilts not only struggle to survive against light, water and dirt; they also have living adversaries just waiting to do damage. *Pets* that have the run of the house may consider your beautiful antique quilt to be their most comfortable resting spot. These animals may have dirt on their paws or fur which can easily transfer to the quilt; they may be harbouring fleas or other insects and in all probability will drool saliva as they sleep. Their claws may snag on fabrics and quilting threads. If you feel you cannot banish your beloved pet from a quilt, try covering the sleeping area with a thick blanket or sheet to help protect it.

There is nothing that nesting *mice* love more than the thick padding inside a quilt – they will not eat these fibres, but will rip apart the surface of a quilt to get at them. If your country house is sometimes visited by mice, you might consider leaving traps under the beds upon which quilts are resting. Keep a stored quilt well-wrapped in a cotton sheet or pillowcase to keep rodents from getting anywhere near it.

Insects will eat protein fibres that can be found in silk or woollen quilts and paddings. The best way to combat this problem is to regularly air and shake out your quilts; vacuuming will go a long way toward removing insect droppings and larvae. If you know that a quilt requires extermination, loosely insert the whole quilt in a large black plastic bag; place a container of paradichlorobenzine mothballs wrapped in acid-free tissue paper on top of the quilt; the vapours will filter downward. Leave undisturbed for a few weeks, then air the quilt thoroughly. Follow this by periodic vacuuming, which will aid in preventing insects from harming the quilt.

Repairing a Quilt

There are many arguments in the quilt world on whether and how an antique quilt should be repaired. People who are interested in quilts primarily for their historical value believe that a quilt should basically be left as it was found – frays, stains and all – because these imperfections are part of its history. Others believe that quilts can be repaired if the work is done sensitively and with respect, by using antique fabrics of the same period or by making the repairs as unobtrusive as possible. Still others believe that antique quilts should be recycled; they feel that if a quilt is frayed and tattered, the deteriorated portion should be cut off and the rest used to make a smaller quilt, cushion or pillow.

If you have a quilt that needs some repairing, the answer is get advice from someone who is very knowledgeable about quilts to see whether the repair you are considering is necessary, or whether there is a way of dealing with it that you haven't previously considered. You may find that certain stains, such as the brown spots that appear on many old quilts, are a result of changes associated with age, and that no amount of washing will get rid of them. What antique quilt collectors must learn to accept is that an old quilt will not look brand-new unless it has been carefully stored and never used. An eagle eye will note that many of the quilts featured in this book are less than perfectly preserved. Part of the charm of an old quilt lies in the fact that it was indeed used by someone – why hide that fact?

Left: A selection of early American quilts rests in a linen press, one of Bob Timberlake's finely crafted reproduction pieces; the chair is upholstered in a Whig's Defeat fabric.

Above: Quilts are a warm, comfortable magnet for pets, but must be safeguarded from claws and fur. Either discourage pets from lying on quilts or cover the quilts with protective fabric.

Professional conservators and museums aim to preserve a quilt's historical value by not removing or concealing any of the fabrics. They do this by stabilizing holes or disintegrating areas with nylon tulle, a polyester fabric called Stabiltex, or a silk fabric called Crepeline. These fabrics will prevent further deterioration but are transparent so that the fabric beneath is still visible. If you wish to repair your own quilt in this way, cut a piece of tulle, Stabiltex or Crepeline slightly larger than the area you wish to cover. Using cotton thread on cotton quilts and silk thread on silk or woollen quilts, secure the covering fabric in place, making the stitches longer than 6mm/¼ in; small stitches will weaken the fabric. Because Crepeline will shred, you'll need to make a narrow hem around the edge before sewing it to the quilt.

If your quilt is damaged and you wish to replace the damaged fabric, try to purchase some antique fabric manufactured around the time your quilt was made. Since antique fabrics are not easy to find, you may need to buy a modern fabric replacement. If this is the case, look for as close a match as possible – both in colour and weave. If the quilt has been washed, prewash the replacement fabric. Rather than remove the damaged fabric, it is better to appliqué the replacement fabric over the damaged area so that the quilt could be returned to its original condition if necessary. When

securing the fabric to the quilt, try to match the way surrounding fabrics have been stitched together. Do not make your stitches too tiny or they may weaken the whole area.

Cutting up old quilts for recycling is anathema to anyone who loves quilts. If you want patchwork cushions or pillows, it is far better to make new ones.

Storage

The quilts that you are not displaying must be stored very carefully because most of the problems associated with displaying a quilt on a bed are magnified when that quilt is stored.

The best way to store a quilt is absolutely flat, unstacked and unfolded, but this is not going to be possible unless you are a professional quilt collector with a lot of ideal storage space. For most quilt collectors, space is at a premium, and *folding* is probably the only option.

Every time a quilt is folded, the fibres along the fold line are placed under pressure. If the quilt is always refolded in the same way, those fibres are eventually going to crack which will cause the fabric to disintegrate. This will also happen if a quilt is left folded in the same position for a long period of time. It is therefore essential that you refold your quilts two or three times a year. Forget about matching corners when you fold – simply try to fold the quilt gently and carefully in a way that it hasn't been folded before. To fold a quilt for storage, crumple acid-free tissue paper into thick wads and place across the quilt before making the first fold. Each time you fold the quilt, pad the fold with acid-free tissue paper; this will help to prevent sharp creases from forming (see the Directory for suppliers of acid-free tissue paper).

Folded quilts may be stored in drawers. Ideally, you should have one quilt per drawer, but few people have that kind of space. Quilts stored in drawers should have as few folds as possible. If the drawers are made of wood or cardboard, line them with acid-free paper or cotton fabric. Once the quilts are in the drawers, cover them with acid-free paper or cotton fabric so that they do not touch the wood or cardboard above.

If you are storing a number of quilts, chances are that you will stack one on top of another. However, the combined weight of a stack of quilts may damage the ones at the bottom of the pile. To eliminate this problem, store folded quilts in acid-free boxes (see the Directory for a list of suppliers). When the quilt has been folded to a size that will fit into the box, first slip it into a cotton pillowcase for added protection, then place the quilt in the box. Be sure to label the box, perhaps giving an indication of when it was last used, aired or folded to aid you in the conservation of your quilt.

If you are only storing one or two quilts and do not wish to use a box, or if your quilts are very light in weight, fold them as described above and slip them into a cotton pillowcase or wrap them securely in a cotton sheet before putting them away in a safe dry place.

Cleaning

Cleaning a quilt should be avoided at all costs. It is much better to preserve and protect your quilt than to make it undergo the stress of wet-washing or dry-cleaning.

Examine your quilt carefully to see whether it really needs to be cleaned or whether it is just covered by surface dust or dirt. If it doesn't look very dirty but has a musty smell, try *airing* it on a windy, dry day to see if that will remove the odour.

If you are still not happy with the quilt, try *vacuuming*. Find a clean square or rectangle of Fibreglass screening and cover the rough edges with fabric or thick tape to prevent any snagging of your quilt. Place the quilt on a large, clean flat surface, or if it is a wall-hanging, keep it on the wall. Set a hand-held vacuum cleaner on its lowest suction power, then, using the upholstery attachment, slowly and gently vacuum the entire surface of the quilt through the Fibreglass screen. Do not allow the fabric to be sucked into the vacuum cleaner; you may need to cover the end of the upholstery attachment with a fine piece of fabric like muslin or cheesecloth.

Turn the quilt over and vacuum the other side in the same manner. Vacuuming your quilts at regular intervals will remove the dust and dirt that can cause the fabrics to degenerate.

However, if vacuuming still doesn't remove all the dirt, you will need to actually clean the quilt. *Dry-cleaning* might seem a safer bet than wet-washing, but it may not be the best method for a fragile quilt because of the strong solvents used. Telephone or visit a local museum and talk with someone in the textile conservation department; ask if they can recommend a dry-cleaner or conservator. Alternatively, try to find a cleaner who specializes in laundering fancy costumes and bridal gowns. When you take your quilt there, specify that you want completely fresh solvent used for cleaning your quilt, and that agitation should be kept to a minimum. Do not expect this process to be inexpensive. Do not dry-clean a quilt that has a white background, or you'll run the risk of yellowing.

Wet-washing is probably a safer method of cleaning an antique quilt, however it is extremely painstaking and time-consuming. Expect to devote at least an entire day to washing one quilt. Also, unless you have a large area inside your home for drying the quilt, wait for a clear, dry day before you start wet-washing. Do not wet-wash a silk or woollen quilt, or a quilt with a combination of textiles like a Crazy quilt. Do not wash a cotton quilt that contains glazed fabrics or disintegrating fibres. Test each of the fabrics in the quilt for colour-fastness: place a drop of tepid water on the fabric and rub gently with a white paper towel; if any of the colour rubs off, do not wash the quilt. Stabilize any holes or disintegrating areas (see p. 136). Also, think very carefully about washing an antique quilt that has never been washed (you can tell if a quilt has been washed because there will be slight puckers between the lines of quilting stitches); you will certainly lessen the quilt's value if you do wash it.

If all of the above conditions are met and you decide to wet-wash your quilt, follow these steps faithfully for the best results. First, thoroughly clean the inside of a large bathtub, then spread a clean, light-coloured sheet inside the bathtub with the edges extending beyond the tub; this sheet will be used for lifting the wet quilt out of the tub when you have finished washing it.

Fill the tub with tepid water, then gently place the quilt in the water, folding it accordian style until all the layers are under the water. Allow the quilt to soak over a twelve-hour period, changing the water periodically without removing the quilt. When draining the tub, make sure the quilt edges are not sucked into the drain. If you feel that the soaking hasn't removed all the dirt, wash the quilt with a mild soap such as Orvus or a neutral detergent. Refill the tub with tepid water, add the soap or detergent and allow the quilt to

soak for about an hour or as recommended on the label. Rinse the quilt with tepid water as many times as necessary until the water runs clear. There should be absolutely no sign of suds in the final rinse. Then, if possible, rinse the quilt again with distilled water. Allow the distilled water to drain out of the tub. Your wet quilt will be quite heavy and the weight of the layers will press out much of the water, so leave the quilt to drain for several hours. While the quilt is draining, cover a dry, shaded area slightly larger than your quilt with towels. Then, with the help of an assistant, gently remove the sheet holding the quilt from the bathtub and carry it to the drying site. Spread the quilt out on the towels, keeping the edges straight and the corners true. Place another layer of thick cotton towels over the quilt and press gently to remove excess moisture. Then remove those towels and cover the quilt with a dry cotton sheet to protect it. It may take more than a day to dry a quilt – especially a thick one. Bring it in at dusk, then repeat the drying process the next day if necessary. Make sure that the quilt is completely dry before storing it.

How to hang a quilt

All quilts that are hung on a wall must be allowed to rest for a time equal to that which they spent hanging. If you buy quilts of a similar size, you can alternate between them, allowing one to rest while the other is on display. Never even consider nailing or tacking a quilt onto a wall, as the nails or tacks will permanently damage the fibres. Sturdy lightweight quilts in good condition can be hung by clips that are nailed to the wall or hung from a line of string or wire. Make sure that you use enough clips – undue pressure on a few spots can cause sagging or even tearing. To protect the quilt at the clipped areas, sandwich the edges with matching fabric. The advantage of clips is that you can remove a quilt and put up a new one easily.

When you hang an antique quilt the weight needs to be evenly distributed along the entire hanging edge, not just a few points. Probably the most popular way of hanging a quilt, and one that is used at most quilt exhibitions, is by inserting a wooden strip through a sleeve or casing of unbleached cotton sewn to the back of the quilt, even when it is being used on a bed. For a newly-made quilt, sew a sleeve in a fabric to match the back.

To make a sleeve, cut a strip of fabric the width of the quilt and 25.4cm/10in wide. Sew a 6mm/¼in hem at each short end, then sew the long edges together making a 13mm/½in seam; press the seam allowance open. Turn the sleeve right side out and press it flat with the seam in the middle of one side. If the sleeve is sewn flat to the back of the quilt, the front will bulge when the wooden strip is inserted; to prevent this, press another crease 13mm/½in away from one of the first creases on the side nearest the seam. Pin the seamed side to the back of the quilt along each of the creases, just below the binding; the free portion of the sleeve will balloon out slightly. Slipstitch each creased edge of the sleeve to the quilt back using cotton or linen thread in a colour to match the quilt. To reduce the stress on the quilt back, make every fourth stitch go through all three layers of the quilt, leaving one stitch showing on the front. Heavy or very wide quilts will need extra support in the middle, such as a bracket, to prevent sagging. In this case, cut the fabric strip for the sleeve in half and finish the short edges with 13mm/½in hems. Make the tubs as above, then sew the sleeves to the quilt back, leaving a 13mm/½in gap in the middle.

Another method of hanging is to use a proprietary closing strip such as Velcro, which will evenly distribute the weight of the quilt as it hangs. Measure the width of the quilt and cut a strip of 5cm/2in -wide Velcro to that length. Also cut a matching strip of 7.6cm/3in -wide cotton twill tape. Cut a wooden lathing strip to the same measurement; sand the wood until smooth and seal with poly-urethane varnish. Machine-sew the fuzzy side of the Velcro to the cotton twill tape. Using cotton or linen thread to match the quilt, hand-sew the twill tape to the top edge of the quilt, just below the binding. To reduce the stress on the quilt back, make every fourth stitch go through all three layers of the quilt, leaving one stitch showing on the front. Never machine-stitch the twill tape to the quilt. Using rustproof staples, staple the hooked side of the Velcro to the lathing strip. Either hang the wooden strip from hooks or nail the strip to the wall in the appropriate position, then simply press the Velcro strips together to hang the quilt.

For greater protection of the fibres and better weight distribution, sew the Velcro to all four edges of the quilt as above. Construct a frame of wooden lathing strips the same size as the quilt, making a lap joint at each corner so that the pieces are flush. Staple the hooked side of the Velcro to the frame, then press the strips together to hang the quilt. Nail the frame to the wall or attach screw eyes to the back and hang it from a wire.

Left: An old painted wooden Swedish blanket chest is home to two colourful turn of the century Log Cabin quilts, which harmonize well with the embroidered wall-hangings (courtesy of Åsa Wettre, Molndahls Museum, Gothenburg, Sweden).

Quilting Patterns

Some of the quilting patterns that follow will need to be enlarged; these have been drawn within a grid of red squares. In order to enlarge the patterns to the correct size, follow the caption that tells you how large the grid should be. For instance, the caption will say: Each square equals 2.54 cm/ 1 in. Tape some sheets of tracing or greaseproof paper together to measure an area slightly larger than the enlarged design will be. Count the number of squares in the grid, then draw the same number of squares on the tracing paper, with each square equal to 2.54 × 2.54 cm/1 × 1 in. Then, holding the drawing in this book next to the new grid, draw the lines of the design onto the new grid, copying each part of the design from the small squares into the large squares.

Trace or enlarge the required quilting patterns and make a template for each as directed on page 149. As a general rule, it is easiest to mark quilting designs on the quilt top before assembling the quilt. To mark a design, place the quilting template on the right side of the fabric and trace around the edge with a sharp hard-lead pencil on light fabrics, or a white dressmaker's pencil on dark fabrics. You can also try using coloured pencils that are slightly darker than the quilt top fabric. After quilting, the lines will be virtually invisible.

For complicated interior design lines, cut narrow channels in the template wide enough to accommodate your pencil. Cut channels only for major interior lines; fill in the remainder freehand, referring back to the lines on the template.

Left: Dramatic red sashing separates the large Evening Star blocks on this 1950s quilt draped over a hickory chair; it was made by Mrs Dorsett in North Carolina.

Left: Corded Trapunto Quilt – Each square 3.5cm/1⅜in

Whig's Defeat

Love Apple

North Country Quilt: Each square 2.54cm/1in

Some traditional quilting patterns

147

Template Patterns

The patterns on the following pages have been grouped together by quilt design (see key below). To save space, the patterns overlap, but you can differentiate between the pieces by looking for the identifying letter inside a bubble along one of the edges. Make a separate tracing for each pattern piece, making sure that you label each one with the appropriate letter. Some of the patterns are larger than the pages of this book. To make the pieces easier to trace, they have been split where they cross the middle of the book. When you are tracing the pieces, first trace the piece on the left-hand page, including the dash lines, then line up your tracing with the dash lines and the edge of the piece on the right-hand page to draw the rest of the pattern.

☐   **Berry Block** *2 patterns (D, E) page 154*
○   **Whig's Defeat** *10 patterns (A-H, M, N) page 154, 155*
⬠   **Pine Burr** *7 patterns (A-G) page 153*
♧   **Autograph Block** *4 patterns (A-D) page 153*
◇   **Crown of Thorns** *12 patterns (A-M) pages 156, 157*
◇   **Spinning Stars** *5 patterns (A-E) page 153*
⬡   **Rose Wreath** *4 patterns (A, B, D, E) page 152*
△   **Heavenly Stars** *6 patterns (A-F) page 155*
○   **Berta Larsson Quilt** *1 pattern (C) page 155*
⌓   **Corded Trapunto Quilt** *1 pattern (A) page 155*
○   **Love Apple** *17 patterns (A-R) pages 158, 159*
        Note: *The letter I is not used to label the pattern pieces.*

Made in Southern Ohio around 1880, this linsey quilt is a 54-40 or Fight design. Linsey fabric was woven in the South during the Civil War when trade with the outside world was greatly reduced.

Above: A carved wooden chair in a traditional Swedish furniture-maker's workshop features two striking Swedish patchwork quilts – a chintz Cotton Reel and a simple woollen Four Patch (courtesy of Åsa Wettre, Molndahls Museum, Gothenburg, Sweden).

Right: An antique Ohio Star quilt made in Sweden to radiate warmth. For extra insulation, it has been sewn onto the woolly side of a sheepskin, the edges of which form a fringe (courtesy of Åsa Wettre, Molndahls Museum, Gothenburg, Sweden).

For tracing instructions see page 149. Many of the patterns shown on the following pages are used to cut hundreds of pieces of fabric and must be made sturdy for repeated use. Therefore, you should make a template for each pattern piece out of durable cardboard or plastic; this holds true when you are making quilting templates. The patchwork and appliqué patterns on these pages do not include a seam allowance. If you are going to hand-sew the pieces, or if you are making appliqué templates, do not add a seam allowance. However, if you are going to machine-sew your patchwork quilt you should add a 6mm/¼in seam allowance all around each template.

Cut out the traced pattern piece and spray-glue it to sturdy cardboard; let the glue dry, then cut out the template using a utility knife. Or, if making plastic templates, trace the outline of the pattern onto the plastic, then cut it out. Be sure to clearly mark the appropriate letter on each template.

For complicated patterns with notches or circles for matching,

mark the notches or circles on the seam line of the tracing, then make a fine cut into the template edges with a utility knife. Mark patchwork pieces one row at a time on the wrong side of the appropriate fabric, providing a mutual cutting edge if possible. The longest edge of each piece should be on the straight grain of the fabric. Mark curved edges on the bias.

For hand-sewing, mark the pieces 13mm/½ inch apart on the wrong side of the fabric to include the seam allowances. Because the templates for machine-sewing already include the seam allowances, mark pieces side-by-side on the wrong side of the fabric for ease in cutting and less wastage. Mark appliqué pieces on the right side of the fabric, leaving a 13mm/½ inch space in between each one. Cut appliqués apart by eye, leaving a 6mm/¼ inch seam allowance all around the edges.

You will be directed to "reserve" some patterns when cutting them out; to do this, simply turn the template over and mark the required number of pieces on the fabric.

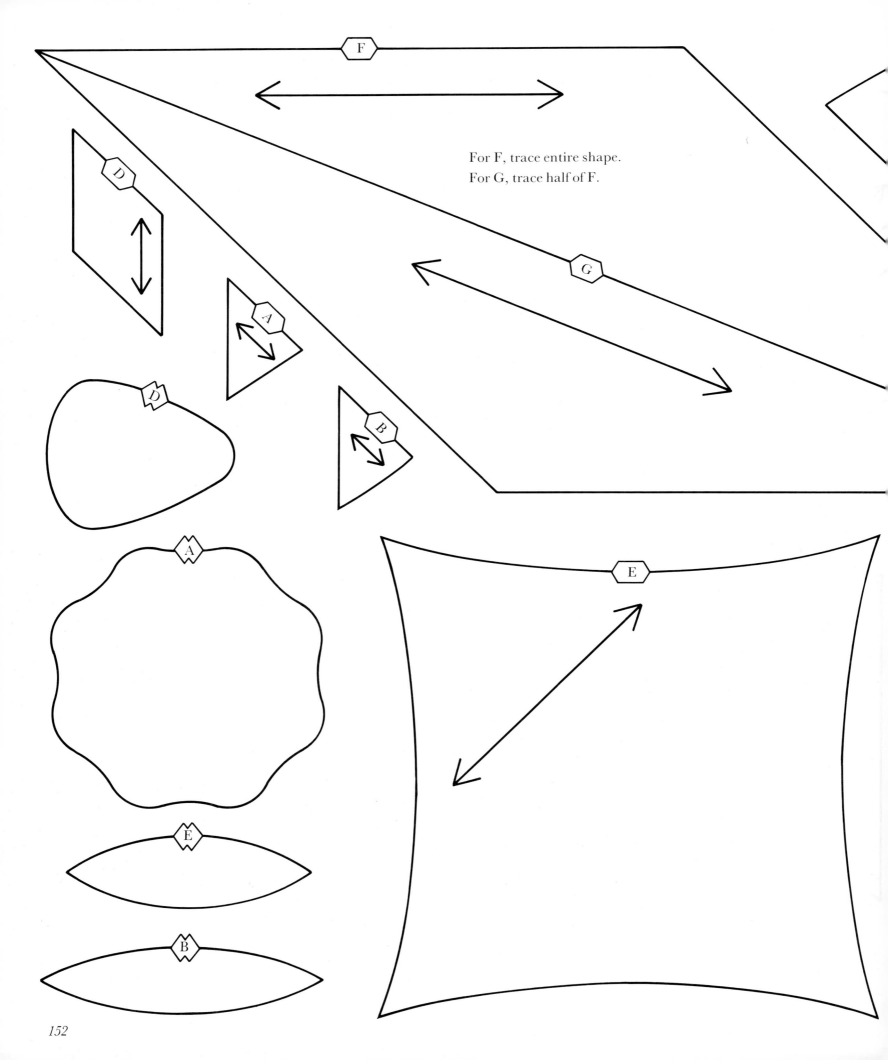

For F, trace entire shape.
For G, trace half of F.

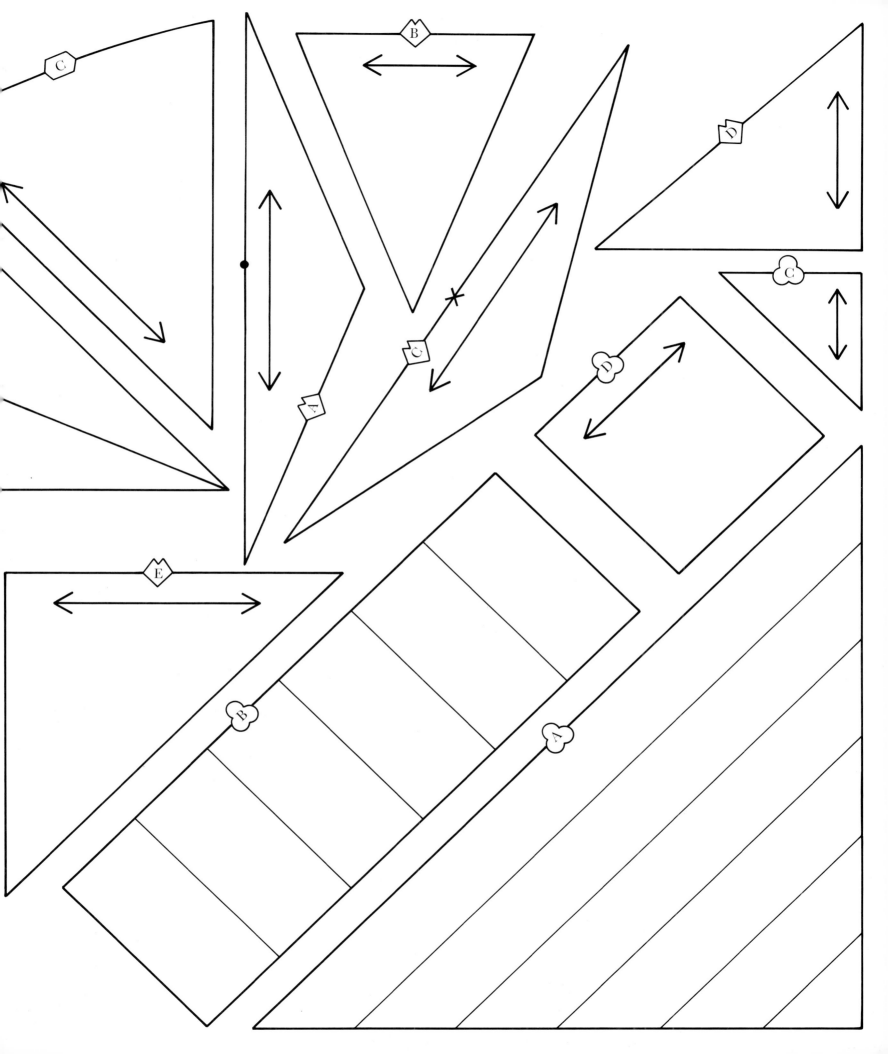

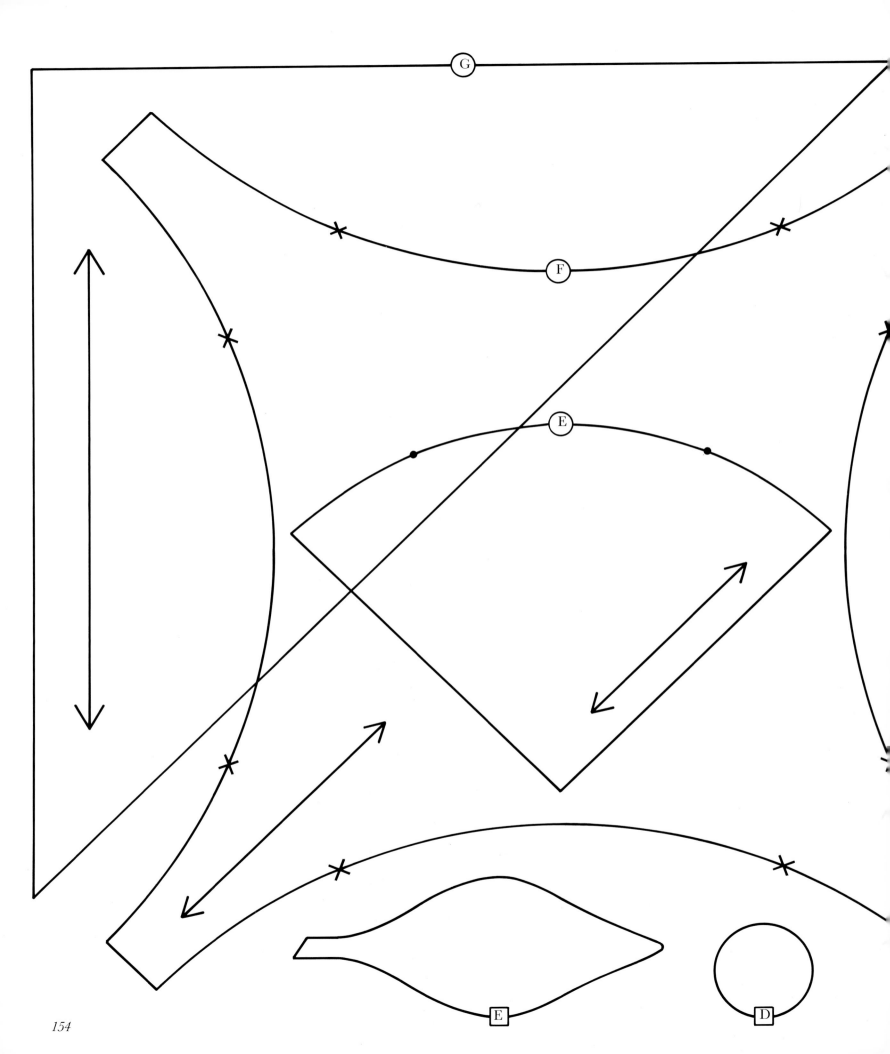

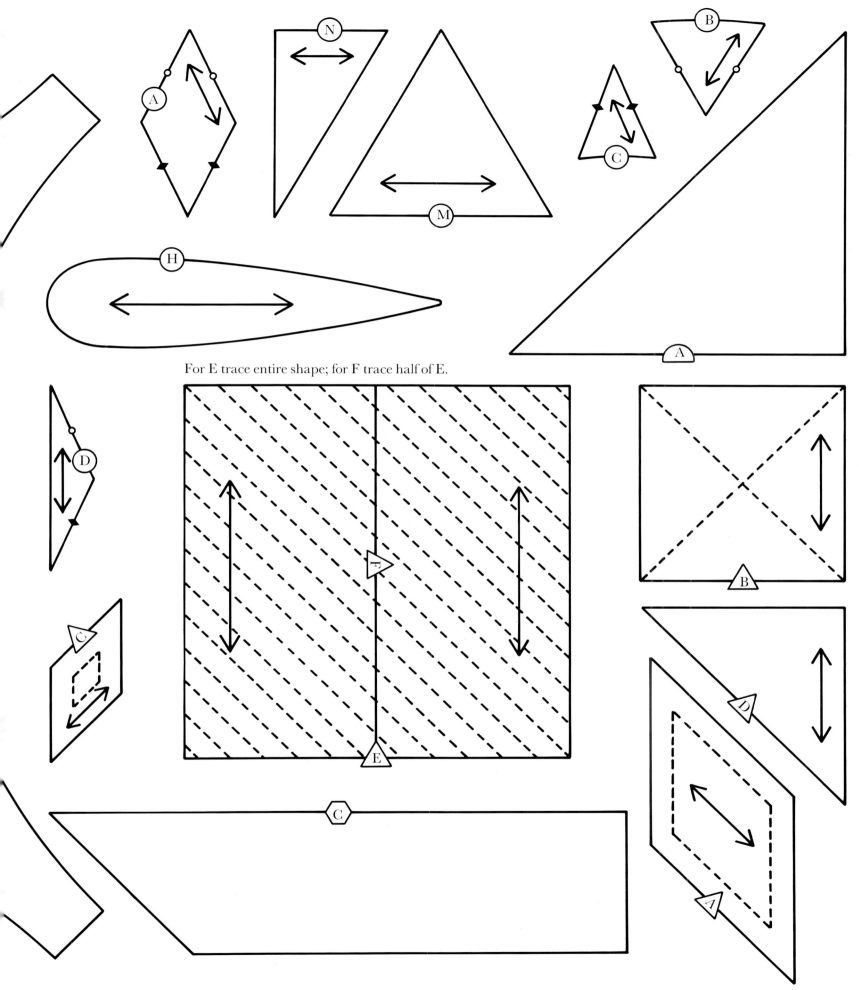

For E trace entire shape; for F trace half of E.

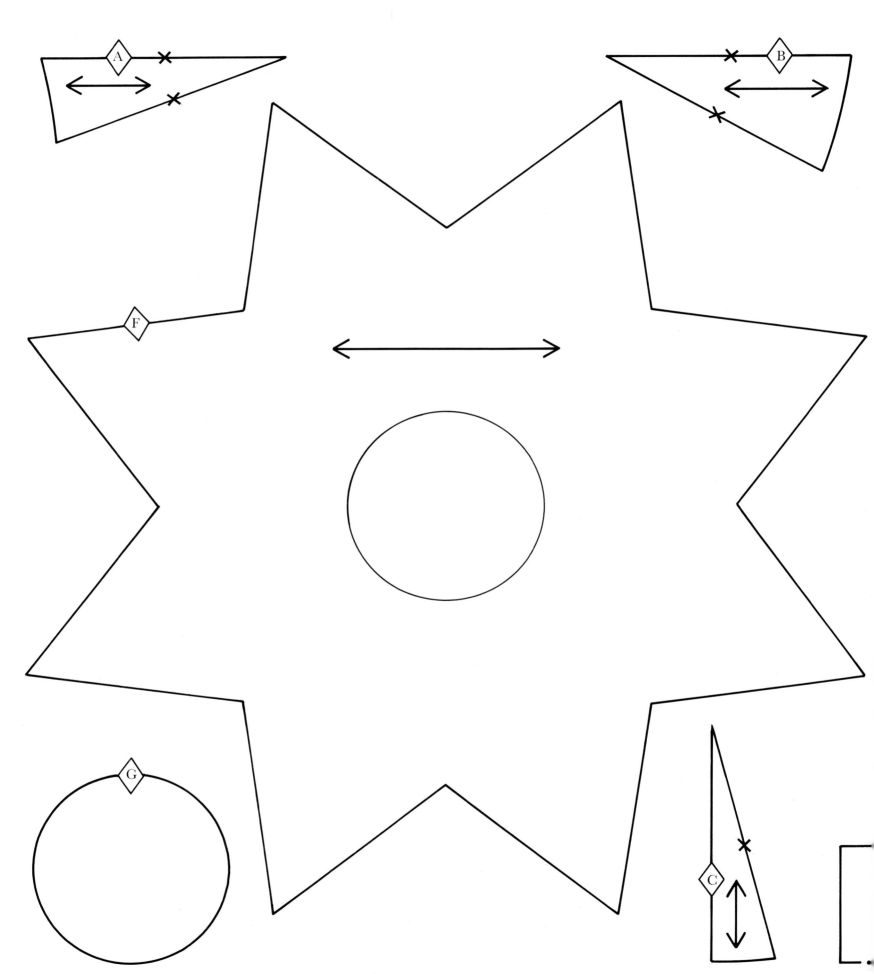

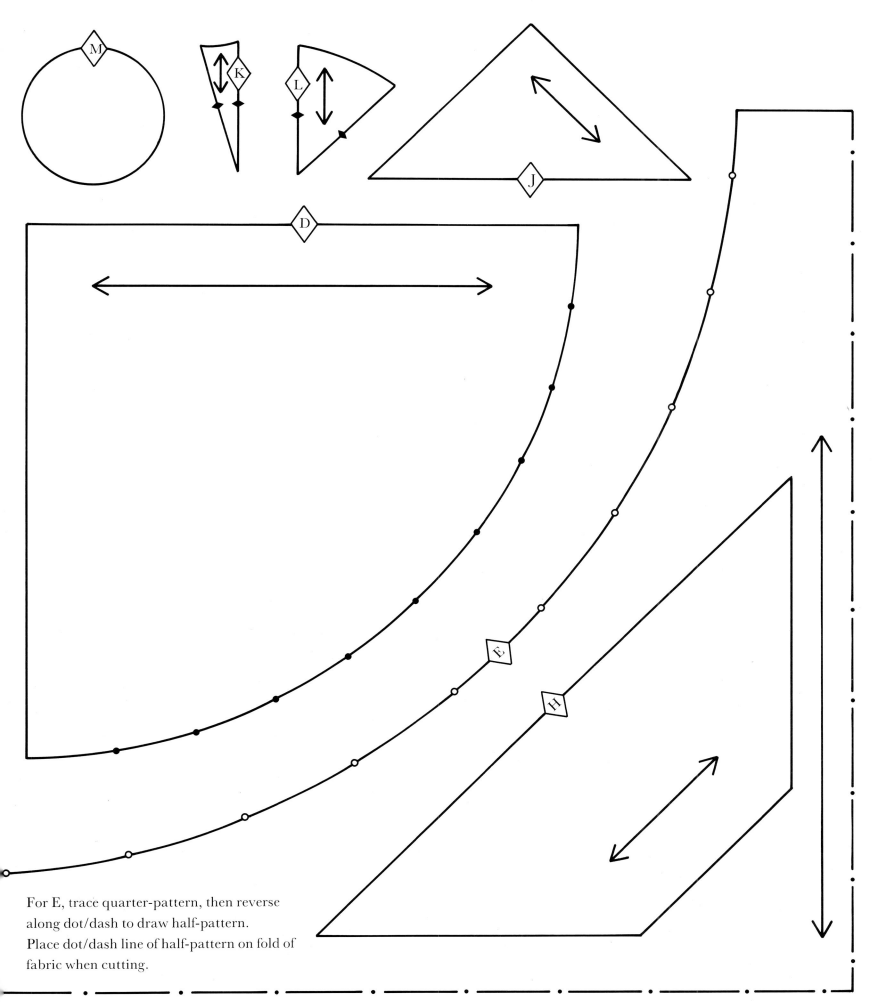

For E, trace quarter-pattern, then reverse
along dot/dash to draw half-pattern.
Place dot/dash line of half-pattern on fold of
fabric when cutting.

159

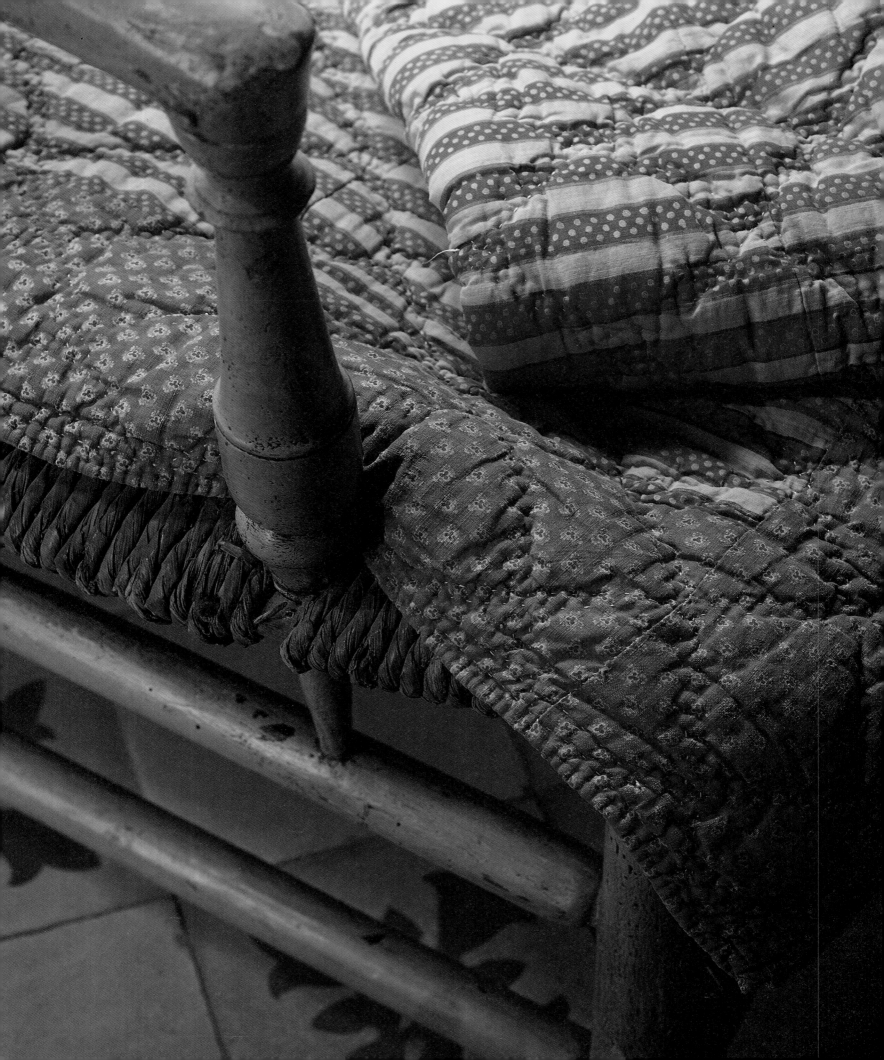

Bibliography

REFERENCE: TEXTILE CARE AND
CONSERVATION

Bogle, Michael. *Textile Conservation Center Notes.*
Merrimack Valley Textile Museum, North
Andover, Massachusetts. 1979.

Finch, Karen and Greta Putnam. *Caring for
Textiles.* Watson–Guptill Publications, New York.
1977.

Korwin, Laurence. *Textiles As Art: Selecting,
Framing, Mounting, Lighting and Maintaining Textile Art.*
Self-published, Chicago, Illinois. 1990.

Landi, Sheila. *A Textile Conservator's Manual.*
Butterworth, London. 1985.

Montgomery, Florence M. *Textiles in America, 1650-
1870.* W.W. Norton & Company, New York. 1984.

O'Bryant Puentes, Nancy. *First Aid for Family
Quilts.* Moon Over the Mountain Publishing
Company, Wheatridge, Colorado. 1986.

Wilson, Max. *A History of Textiles.* Westview Press,
Boulder, Colorado. 1979.

PERIODICALS: TEXTILE CARE AND
CONSERVATION

*Chemical Spots, Stains and Discoloration of Textile Home
Furnishings,* American Textile Manufacturers
Institute, Washington, D.C. n.d. (pamphlet).

Division of Textiles, Smithsonian Institution.
An Introduction to Textile Conservation. The National
Museum of American History, Washington, D.C.,
1976 (pamphlet).

Division of Textiles, Smithsonian Institution.
The Care and Cleaning of Antique Cotton and Linen Quilts.
The National Museum of History and Technology,
Washington, D.C. n.d. (pamphlet).

Division of Textiles, Smithsonian Institution.
Care of Victorian Silk Quilts and Slumberthrows. National
Museum of American History, Washington, D.C.,
n.d. (pamphlet).

Division of Textiles, Smithsonian Institution.
Mounting Flat Textile Objects Using Velcro. The
National Museum of American History,
Washington, D.C., n.d. (pamphlet).

Gunn, Virginia. *The Display, Care, and Conservation of
Old Quilts,* In the Heart of Pennsylvania Symposium
Papers. The Oral Traditions Project of the Union
County Historical Society, Lewisburg,
Pennsylvania, 1986.

Gunn, Virginia. *New Thoughts on Care and Conservation,*
In the Heart of Pennsylvania Symposium Papers.
The Oral Traditions Project of the Union County
Historical Society, Pennsylvania, 1991.

Orlofsky, Patsy. *The Collector's Guide for the
Care of Quilts in the Home,* Quilt Digest 2, Kiracofe and
Kile, San Francisco, California, 1984.

REFERENCE: QUILTS

Barker, Vicki and Tessa Bird. *The Fine Art of
Quilting.* Studio Vista, London. 1990.

Betterton, Sheila. *Quilts and Coverlets.* The American
Museum in Britain, Bath. 1978.

Bishop, Robert and Carter Houck. *All Flags
Flying: American Patriotic Quilts as Expressions of Liberty.*
E P Dutton, New York. 1986.

Bishop, Robert and Elizabeth Safanda. *A Gallery
of Amish Quilts.* E P Dutton & Co, New York. 1976.

Brackman, Barbara. *Clues in the Calico.* EPM
Publications, Inc., McLean, Virginia. 1989.

Colby, Averil. *Patchwork.* B T Batsford, London.
1958.

Colby, Averil. *Quilting.* Charles Scribner's Sons,
New York. 1971.

Cooper, Patricia and Norma Bradley Allen. *The
Quilters: Women and Domestic Art.* Doubleday, New
York. 1989.

DePauw, Linda Grant and Conover Hunt.
Remember the Ladies: Women in America 1750-1815. The
Viking Press, New York. 1976.

Duke, Dennis and Deborah Harding (editors).
America's Glorious Quilts. Park Lane, New York. 1987.

Bibliography

Ferrero, Pat and Elaine Hedges, Julie Silber. *Hearts and Hands: The Influence of Women & Quilts on American Society.* The Quilt Digest Press, San Francisco, California. 1987.

Finley, Ruth. *Old Patchwork Quilts and the Women Who Made Them.* J.B. Lippincott Company, Philadelphia. 1929.

Fitzrandolph, Mavis. *Traditional Quilting.* B. T. Batsford Ltd, London. 1954.

Granick, Eve Wheatcroft. *The Amish Quilt.* Good Books, Intercourse, Pennsylvania. 1989.

Hall, Carrie A. and Rose G. Kretsinger. *The Romance of the Patchwork Quilt in America.* Bonanza Books, New York. 1935.

Hinson, Dolores A. *Quilting Manual.* Dover Publications, Inc, New York. 1966, 1970.

Holstein, Jonathan. *The Pieced Quilt.* New York Graphic Society Press, Greenwich, Connecticut. 1974.

Hornung, Clarence P.
Treasury of American Design:
A Pictorial Survey of Popular Folk Arts.
Harry N. Abrams, New York. 1971.

Houck, Carter. *The Quilt Encyclopedia Illustrated.* Harry N. Abrams, Inc., New York. 1991.

Ickis, Marguerite. *The Standard Book of Quiltmaking & Collecting.* Dover Publications, Inc, New York. 1949.

Jenkins, Susan and Linda Seward. *Quilts: The American Story.* Harper Collins, London. 1991.

Khin, Yvonne M. *The Collector's Dictionary of Quilt Names & Patterns.* Acropolis Books Ltd, Washington, D.C. 1980.

Lasansky, Jeannette. *In the Heart of Pennsylvania: 19th & 20th Century Quiltmaking Traditions.* Oral Traditions Project, Lewisburg, Pennsylvania. 1985.
Pieced by Mother: Over 100 Years of Quiltmaking Traditions. Oral Traditions Project, Pennsylvania. 1987.

Lipman, Jean, and Alice Winchester. *The Flowering of American Folk Art, 1776-1876.* Viking Press, New York. 1974.

Lipsett, Linda Otto. *Remember Me: Women & Their Friendship Quilts.* The Quilt Digest Press, San Francisco. 1985.

Martin, Nancy J. *Pieces of the Past.* That Patchwork Place, Inc., Bothell, Washington. 1986.

Orlofsky, Patsy and Myron. *Quilts in America.* McGrawHill Book Company, New York. 1974.

Osler, Dorothy. *Traditional British Quilts.* B. T. Batsford, Ltd., London. 1987.

Payne, Suzzy Chalfant and Susan Aylsworth Murwin. *Creative American Quilting Inspired by the Bible.* Fleming H. Revell Company, New Jersey. 1983.

Pettit, Florence H. *America's Printed and Painted Fabrics 1600-1900.* Hastings House, New York. 1970.

Peto, Florence. *American Quilts and Coverlets.* Chanticleer Press, New York. 1949.

Rae, Janet. *The Quilts of the British Isles.* Bellew Publishing, London. 1987.

Ramsey, Bets and Merikay Waldvogel. *The Quilts of Tennessee.* Rutledge Hill Press, Nashville, Tennessee. 1986.

Safford, Carleton L and Robert Bishop. *America's Quilts and Coverlets.* E P Dutton & Company, Inc., New York. 1980.

Waldvogel, Merikay. *Soft Covers for Hard Times: Quiltmaking & The Great Depression.* Rutledge Hill Press, Nashville, Tennessee. 1990.

Webster, Marie D. *Quilts: Their Story and How to Make Them.* Tudor Publishing Company, New York. 1915.

Weissman, Judith Reiter, and Wendy Lavitt. *Labors of Love: America's Textiles and Needlework, 1650-1930.* Alfred A. Knopf, New York. 1987.

QUILTMAKING TECHNIQUES

Conroy, Mary. *The Complete Book of Crazy Patchwork.* Sterling Publishing Company, Inc., New York. 1985.

Emms MBE, Amy. *Amy Emms' Story of Durham Quilting.* Search Press Limited, Tunbridge Wells, Kent. 1990.

Gutcheon, Beth. *The Perfect Patchwork Primer.* Penguin Books Ltd, Harmondsworth, England. 1973.

James, Michael. *The Quiltmaker's Handbook.* PrenticeHall, Inc, New Jersey. 1978. *The Second Quiltmaker's Handbook.* Prentice-Hall, 1981.

Leone, Diana. *Fine Hand Quilting.* Leone Publications, Los Altos, California. 1986.

Macho, Linda. *Quilting Patterns.* Dover Publications, Inc, New York. 1984.

Morgan, Mary and Dee Mosteller. *Trapunto and Other Forms of Raised Quilting.* Charles Scribner's Sons, New York. 1977.

Seward, Linda. *The Complete Book of Patchwork Quilting and Appliqué.* Mitchell Beazley, London. 1987. *Small Quilting Projects,* Sterling Publishing Company, Ltd, New York, 1987.

Directory

HOME CARE AND CONSERVATION OF ANTIQUE QUILTS

UK

Atlantis Paper Company, Ltd.
2 Saint Andrews Way
London
E3 3PA
Range of acid-free products and storage boxes.

Falkiner Fine Papers Ltd.
76 Southampton Row
London
WC1 4AR
Range of acid-free paper products.

Hepden & Co., Ltd.
Unit 9/10, Rich
Industrial Estate
Crimscott Street
London
SE1 5TE
Velcro and general haberdashery.

Holman & Williams
H & W House
Riverside Road
Wimbledon
London
SW17 0BA
Acid-free tissue paper; storage tubes.

Plastok Associates, Ltd.
79 Market Street
Birkenhead
Wirral
Merseyside
L41 6AN
Stabiltex fabric and other fine nets.

Preservation Equipment, Ltd.
Church Road
Shelfanger
Diss
Norfolk
IP22 2DG
Range of Acid-free products.

Progressive Paper
18 Crawford Place
London
W1
Acid-free paper.

Protectafilm
Unit 6
Twyford Business
Centre
London Road
Bishops Stortford
Herts
CM23 3YT
Solar control UV window films for protection against the effects of light.

Solar Shield, Ltd.
Gray's Farm Road
Unit 11
St. Paul's Cray
Kent
BR5 3BD
Solar control film and blinds for protection against the effects of light.

USA

Archivart
7 Caesar Place
PO Box 428
Moonachie
NJ 07074
Suppliers of conservation materials – acid-free tissue paper, rolling tubes and storage boxes.

Clotilde, Inc.
1909 SW First Avenue
Fort Lauderdale
FL 33315-2100
Orvus, and other supplies such as 100% cotton batting.

Conservation Materials, Ltd.
1165 Marietta Way
Box 2884
Sparks
NV 89431
Conservation materials, including Orvus paste and liquid detergent; silk Crepeline; acid-free tissue paper, storage boxes and rolling tubes; linen thread.

Solar Screen Co., Inc.
53-11 105th Street
Corona
NY 11368
UV film and fluorescent bulb jackets.

TALAS
213 West 35th Street
New York
NY 10001-1996
*Acid-free tissue paper and storage boxes; silk thread; adhesive web; Crepeline; Orvus paste.
Will also perform conservation work on quilts.*

AUSTRALIA

Edwards, Dunlop & Ball
121 Beaufort Street
Preston
Victoria 3072
Acid-free tissue paper, rolling tubes and storage boxes.

FRANCE

Paul L G Dulac & Ore
3 Rue Roman
5 Place du Griffon
Lyons
France
Silk Crepeline.

GERMANY

Klassen Papertronics KG
Landsbergerstrasse 80
D-4300
Essen-Kettwig
Acid-free tissue paper, rolling tubes and storage boxes.

IRELAND

William Clarke & Sons Ltd.
Upperlands-Maghera
County Londonderry
NI BT46 5RZ
Linen fabric.

SWITZERLAND

Swiss Silk Bolting Cloth Manufacturing Co., Ltd.
Grutlestrasse 68
CH 8002 Zurich
Polyester Crepeline; Stabiltex.

CONSERVATION AND RESTORATION OF ANTIQUE QUILTS

UK

The Conservation Unit
Museums & Galleries
Commission
16 Queen Anne's Gate
London SW1H 9AA
Gives conservation advice and support to both public and private sectors; for small fee, will provide database search facility for a listing of specialist conservators.

The Textile Conservation Centre, Ltd.
Apt. 22
Hampton Court Palace
East Molesey
Surrey
KT8 9AU
Private organization that provides conservation services as well as training courses for textile conservators.

Victoria & Albert Museum
(Textile Conservation Department)
Brompton Road
South Kensington
London
SW7 2RL
*Will examine and advise on antique textile conservation and restoration.
Some museum staff will also undertake private commissions.*

Jenny Band
Textile Conservation
Studio
Apt 37
Lord Chamberlain
Court
Hampton Court Palace
East Molesey
Surrey
KT8 9AU
Will give conservation condition reports and perform conservation and restoration work.

Judith Doré & Bernard Doré
Castle Lodge
271 Sandown Road
Deal
Kent
CT14 6QU
Conservators; solvent cleaning and wetwashing of historic textiles.

Debbie Williams
23A Cumberland Street
Pimlico
London SW1
Conservation and restoration work.

USA

Conservation Referral Service
Foundation of the
American Institute for
Conservation
of Historic & Artistic
Works
1400 16th Street, NW
Suite 340
Washington
DC 20036
Free referral service for conservators or restorers by speciality.

Directory

Martha Grimm
4347 East North Lane
Phoenix
AZ 82502
Conservation and restoration work.

Nancy Sloper Howard
The Textile Conservation Workshop
3538 Digger Pine Ridge
Winters
CA 95694
Conservation and restoration work.

Patsy Orlofsky
The Textile Conservation Workshop, Inc.
Main Street
South Salem
NY 10590
Provides all conservation and restoration services. Also undertakes cleaning and valuations.

Betsey Telford
Rocky Mountain Quilts
3847 Alt. 6 & 24
Palisade
CD 81526
Restoration and sale of antique quilts.

Texas Conservation Center
The Panhandle-Plains Historical Museum
PO Box 967
W.T. Station
Canyon
TX 79016
Conservation and restoration work.

Gloria White
2 Ocean Avenue
Rockport
MA 01966
Restoration and sale of antique quilts.

SWEDEN

Lena Engquist
Arme Museum
Stockholm
Sweden
Conservation and restoration work.

SWITZERLAND

Annette Beentyes
Museum of Art & History
Geneva
Conservation and restoration work.

ANTIQUE QUILTS FOR SALE

UK

Antique Textile Company
100 Portland Road
London
W11 4LQ
English and French antique quilts.

Judy Greenwood Antiques
657 Fulham Road
London
SW6 5PY
English, French and some American quilts.

Tricia Jameson Design
Chelsea Green
29 Elystan Street
London
SW3 3NT
Early English and American quilts. Also stocks English, French and American country antiques.

Susan Jenkins
Museum Quilts Gallery
3rd Floor
254-258 Goswell Road
London
EC1V 7EB
Over 300 American quilts from 1800 to the 1930s; catalogue available.

Ron Simpson
Portobello Road
London
W11
Welsh quilts.

Tobias and the Angel
White Hart Lane
Barnes
London
SW13
British quilts and antiques.

USA

America Hurrah Antiques
766 Madison Avenue
New York
NY 10021

June Blackburn
4148 South Norfolk
Tulsa
Oklahoma
74105

M. Finkel & Daughter
936 Pine Street
Philadelphia
PA 19107

Laura Fisher Antique Quilts
Gallery 57
1050 Second Avenue
New York
NY 10022

The Gazebo of New York
660 Madison Avenue
New York
NY 10021
Antique and modern quilts.

Great Expectations Quilts, Inc.
14520 Memorial
Suite 54
Houston
TX 77079
Antique and contemporary quilts.

Oh, Suzanna
16 South Broadway
Lebanon
OH 45036
Quilts and country antiques.

Old Country Store
Main Street
Intercourse
PA 17534
Antique and reproduction Amish and Mennonite quilts.

Quilts Unlimited
440a Duke of Gloucester Street
Williamsburg
VA 22901
Antique and contemporary quilts. A catalogue is available.

Stella Rubin Antiques
12300 Glen Road
Potomac
Maryland
20854
Quilts, baskets and country antiques.

AUSTRALIA

Annette Gero
4 Rangers Road
Cremorne
Sydney
NSW 2090
American patchwork and appliqué quilts.

FURNITURE AND ACCESSORIES

UK

Tricia Jameson Design
Chelsea Green
29 Elystan Street
London
SW3 3NT
Interior decorator specializing in English, French and American country-style antiques.

Mary Wondrausch
The Pottery
Brickfields
Compton
nr. Guildford
Surrey
GU3 1HZ
Commemorative slipware pottery.

USA

Heart's Ease
4101 Burton Drive
Cambria CA
Baskets; dried flowers; herbs and spices; garden accessories.

Tasha Polizzi
T.P. Saddle Blanket & Trading Co.
304 Main Street
Great Barrington
MA 01230
Adirondack-style twig beds; Indian blankets and rugs; Indian baskets; gypsy willow furniture from Arkansas.

Laura Ann Rau
Atascosita Antiques
1124 Milam Street
Columbus
TX 78934
American antiques and English pottery.

Bob Timberlake
The Heritage Company Inc. of Lexington
PO Box 1027
Lexington
NC 27293-1027
Reproduction country-style furniture, accessories, quilts, bedding.

MISCELLANEOUS

Craft Publications
Marsh Mills
Luck Lane
Marsh
Huddersfield
West Yorkshire
HD3 4AB
England
Subscription service for American quilting magazines and books.

National Patchwork Association
PO Box 300
Hethersett
Norwich
Norfolk
NR9 3DB
England
Membership includes quarterly magazine, The Independent Patchworker.

The Quilters Guild
OP66 Dean Clough
Halifax
West Yorkshire
HX3 5AX
England
Membership includes access to their library and quarterly magazine, The Quilter.

Patchwork & Quilting
1 Highfield Close
Malvern Link
Worcs
WR14 1SH
England
British quarterly quilting magazine.

USA

Lady's Circle Patchwork Quilts
111 East 35th Street
New York
NY 10016
American bi-monthly quilting magazine.

Quilter's Newsletter Magazine
Box 394
Wheatridge
CL 80034-0394
American monthly quilting magazine.

Quiltmaker
Box 394
Wheatridge
CL 80034 9917
American quarterly quiltmaking pattern magazine.

Quilts & Other Comforts
PO Box 3942
Wheatridge
CL 80034-0394
Catalogue of quilting products, patterns and magazines.

SWEDEN

Åsa Wettre
Carl Skottbergsgata 38 A
S-413 19 Göteborg
Sweden
Large collection of antique Swedish quilts for exhibition purposes; her book, "Old Swedish Quilts" will be published by Tidens förlag, Warfvinges väg 16, Box 30 184, S-104 25 Stockholm, Sweden in 1993.

Index

MUSEUMS DISPLAYING QUILTS

FRANCE

Souleaido Museum,
Tarascon,
Provence
Owned by the world-famous fabric company, this museum displays their collection of Provençal boutis.

USA

Adirondack Museum,
Bull Cottage,
Blue Mountain Lake,
NY 12812
Cabins built for the rich at the turn of the century, now a unique museum of period holiday retreats.

Atlanta Historical Society,
3101 Andrews Drive,
NW,
Atlanta,
Georgia 30305
Collection of houses representing the historical heritage of the region.

Museum of Appalachia,
Norris,
Tennessee
Folk and country artefacts.

SWEDEN

Molndahls Museum,
Gothenburg
Collection devoted to Swedish country furniture and way of life.

Acknowledgments

A book may only have one or two names on the front cover, but it is always a cooperative effort involving many people. I would like to thank James Merrell for taking such sensitive and splendid photographs – the quilts and their settings benefitted greatly from his talented eye. The book's designers, Jacqui Small and Larraine Lacey, played a big part in making the book look as wonderful as it does. And my editor, Judith More, has done a commendable job, not the least part of which was putting up with a very cantankerous author. Many thanks to Kevin Hart, who painted the beautiful watercolours of the quilts, and to Kuo Kang Chen who took such care in drawing the templates. Thanks also to Catherine Smith and Jaspal Bhangra.

I would like to thank the following people who made writing this book possible on a personal level. Susanna Cassel went above and beyond the duties of an *au pair* in the final weeks of writing this book while she basically took over the running of my house and the care of my daughters. Two kind friends took over my school car pool duties to enable me to write all day without interruption: I'm very grateful to Jackie Bowden and Sheila Madhvani, and also to Louise Hackett, who helped in other ways. Many thanks to Annlee Landman who provided her usual moral support; she also prepared the Directory for me. Susan Jenkins proved to be an invaluable friend and colleague – from loaning her quilts for photography to providing me with hard-to-find books and articles on quilt care and display. Merikay Waldvogel loaned her quilts and her home for photography and supplied me with excellent background information on each of her quilts; she and her husband were also very kind to James Merrell and Jacqui Small while they were in Tennessee. Ursula Stürzinger was extremely helpful to me in the early stages of this book, as was Rosie Macho.

In addition, I'd like to thank the following people who loaned their quilts, their homes or museums or both for the photography in this book: The Adirondack Museum in New York State; The Museum of Appalachia in Norris, Tennessee; Atlanta Historical Society; Celine Bocsset of the Musee Charles Demery in Tarascon, France; Dame Elisabeth Frink and Alex Czaki; Tricia Jameson of Jameson Design; Sharon L. Lovejoy of Heartsease; Marie Louise Olsen and The Molndals Museum in Sweden; Bill and Angela Page; Jack and Tasha Polizzi; Laura Ann and Buddy Rau; Ron Simpson; Steve Regan and Bob Timberlake; Åsa Wettre and Mary Wondrausch.

Finally, I'd like to thank my husband, Robert, who is always there with ideas, alternatives and calming influences when I need them most.